Feeling Fate

Feeling Fate

A Memoir of Love, Intuition, and Spirit

Joni Sensel

SHE WRITES PRESS

Published 2022
Printed in the United States of America
Print ISBN: 978-1-64742-339-1
E-ISBN: 978-1-64742-340-7
Library of Congress Control Number: 2021916465

For information, address:
She Writes Press
1569 Solano Ave #546
Berkeley, CA 94707

She Writes Press is a division of SparkPoint Studio, LLC.

All company and/or product names may be trade names, logos, trademarks, and/or registered trademarks and are the property of their respective owners.

Names and identifying characteristics have been changed to protect the privacy of certain individuals.

For Tony, of course.
But also for Jo Anna.

"There are more things in heaven and earth, Horatio, than are dreamt of in our philosophy."

—Hamlet, *The Tragedy of Hamlet* (First Folio), Act 1, Scene 5

My own suspicion is that the universe is not only queerer than we suppose, but queerer than we *can* suppose.

—J.B.S. Haldane, scientist

PART 1

THEN

My Secret

My dearest Tony,

You'd been gone a couple of hours, but your body was still here. All six-foot-two of you stretched out on the living room floor on the sheet the paramedics had used to carry you downstairs. They'd banged your big feet and shoulders against the wall and balustrade. As I followed them, I'd looked away. Pretended not to hear that clunking. Now I was crouched on the step stool in the kitchen, clutching my robe around me and trying not to see your husk from the corner of my eye. Your essence clung more to the kitchen cabinets you'd installed, the slate gray appliances we'd picked out together, the wood grain flooring you'd removed and replaced. But it's a small house we shared, so your face loomed pale in my peripheral vision.

I hunkered over my knees, my position upright but fetal. I needed to be close to the floor. Where it's hard to fall down. The floor your body was laid out on. It kept us together. I considered slipping down to the cold laminate and curling into myself there. Its chill seemed inviting. But I didn't want to make the volunteer EMTs, mostly strangers, any more uncomfortable than they already looked.

They'd tried hard. For an hour. After my own thirty minutes of CPR on your chest. They were kind. Several lingered until Mom or the medical examiner could arrive so I didn't have to wait by myself. You were gone. In the meantime, I had to make myself small, low to the ground, so the Universe wouldn't notice me there. It had made a bargain with me, and the price had come due, but the real pain hadn't hit yet. If I stayed small, maybe I could keep the pain smaller, too.

Mom and Dad arrived, sliding open the door. A puff of cold came in with them, the air chilled by the two feet of snow on the ground. I looked up but stayed down, my wrists pressed to my chest.

Mom bent toward me. "I'm so sorry, honey." She probably put an arm around me. I don't remember.

Tears choked my voice. "I've always known I wouldn't have him for long."

She straightened. "How did you know?"

She probably expected to hear of some illness, some diagnosis you'd had. There hadn't been one. The paramedics had not wanted to believe the bottle of aspirin in the kitchen windowsill was there for our two arthritic dogs, not so you could thin your blood or treat splitting headaches. They asked over and over when I told them the truth.

Their persistence stirred a childhood wound—aspirin and I have an ugly history—but I understood why they kept asking. Nobody likes the grim fact that a strong, athletic man of fifty-nine might die in his sleep, without the slightest warning, at 4:45 in the morning. Your only health complaints were knees worn down by football and an old shoulder injury stirred by the lifting you'd done to single-handedly build dormers onto our house. You didn't even carry the typical American's spare twenty pounds. We'd pumped iron at our local gym twelve hours earlier. We'd made love in front of the fire before heading upstairs to bed.

But when Mom asked how I knew our time would be short, I shrugged through my tears. "I don't know. Pre-birth contract?" The truth was too complicated to push out while weeping.

So I'm telling you instead, sweetheart. We never talked about this, though it was on my mind often. I tried once to share this secret.

But my bargain with the Universe was hard to bring up. It seemed presumptuous to suggest I'd made a divine bargain for you as though you had no say in our love. You were too self-possessed, too powerful a man for me to claim such a thing. Even if I knew it was true.

More importantly, I was afraid to give my intuition weight. To put it in words. If I never said what I knew, maybe it wouldn't come true. Better yet, perhaps I was wrong, a kook for believing divine forces made bargains.

Your death three years later confirmed my worst fears . . . while sliding rebar into the intuitions that form my spiritual faith. I'm put in the strange position of having lost the one thing in my life—you— that had convinced me of a benevolent Universe of wonder and love. And yet your loss and our fairy-tale romance are also my best proof of spiritual truths—a capital-I Infinite, divine forces of fate. If I'm to survive, I have to cling to that rebar. Searing or not, it reminds me that a grander reality exists. My heart knew the truth, and I have to keep trusting it. Through and beyond the despair of my grief.

I can no longer touch you or smell your scent on your pillow. My intuition, that most maligned of the senses, is the only one I can lean on to keep your love close. As far as I know, there were no other secrets between us. Please let me share this one with you now: all the hints that accumulated on my big premonition, like coral building a reef. They added up to my knowing. You gave me evidence you knew it, too, which kept us honeymooning for nearly four years. That internal wisdom deserves to be honored. I have to explain what my heart knew, and how.

PART 2

BEFORE

Insight

You first caught my attention in the St. Maarten airport. We were both wandering the gates, hours early for a gathering of strangers who would board a charter flight to Dominica. Never good at sitting and giddy on novelty, I explored corners like a curious lion cub, watching the antics of other travelers and peering out every window to imagine a life in that exotic location. On my third lap of the gates, you crossed my path.

Your red gear bag did not have a scuba sticker on it. Your build—tall and broad-shouldered and athletic—and the salty streaks in your hair were my only clues. Still, I thought, "He looks like a diver. I bet he's part of our group."

Ten points: I was right. The energy between us was already sparking, the Universe pointing you out in the crowd.

Our group gathered at a gate but without time to swap names. By the time we reached our divers' hotel, it was dark. When we clustered on the patio for group introductions, you were merely the tallest shadow in the tropical air. You mentioned you were married, perhaps marking yourself off limits in a group dominated by single women. We were all there to dive, not to find romance, but people can't help themselves. Not when their dive buddy is so good-looking.

But I also suspect you were feeling guilty. Your wife lay nearly lifeless in the last throes of young-onset Alzheimer's. After years of caregiving, you'd let your sisters convince you that you couldn't let

Lynetta's disease end your life, too. You'd followed an old dream and taken up diving. This week in Dominica was your second trip.

Knowing you were married made you easier for me to talk to—with less distraction from your square jaw or cute, gap-toothed smile. The next day at breakfast, our group learned that you were an assistant manager at GM's Corvette plant in Bowling Green, Kentucky.

One of the other men in our group, a dentist, commented on the prestige of a job building sports cars.

Instead of basking, you made fun of the brand's mystique. "It's a *car*," you said, laughing. "It gets you from Point A to Point B."

I'd later see how proud you really were of your work. You described yourself as a teen jock and a crummy student, but you'd climbed from your first job, sweating over hot machines with headliner foam clinging to your skin, through the assembly line and union leadership into management. Your work gave me fodder for conversation. My work as a freelance writer for big corporations had taught me a lot about manufacturing, and assembly lines have always fascinated me, so we had something to talk about in addition to diving.

At lunchtime I asked you questions about GM and the union, chasing off other divers who'd lingered after the meal. You moved into the empty seat opposite mine. To be closer? Watching you as we chatted under the awning, I had an overwhelming intuition. I'm usually awful at reading other people, but this insight came easy: You needed a friend. It rolled off you to me in waves that were nearly tangible. I didn't know yet why you felt so alone, nothing at all about your wife's situation, but the impression was strong and, I'm sure, involuntary.

You would've been ashamed of that need, wouldn't you? Or considered it a weakness revealed to a stranger. I never mentioned it because I realized pretty quickly that if I did, you'd have wondered who else might have seen it.

Well, okay, I thought. *I can be a friend.*

Who was this man I'd gained this sixth sense about, when I'm normally the last in the room to hear subtext? I began to study you from afar.

What I Noticed about You

1 **Hot**. Between dives, you and the other guys peeled off your wetsuits in the sun. Hiding behind my reflective sunglasses, I admired a man in his fifties in such good shape—but safe. Married. Apparently I'm in the minority, but I would never cross that line. I wouldn't help anyone betray a wife, having been one. And after watching a friend waste too many years pining for a married and disloyal jerk, I would never do it to myself, either. It's not worth the grief.

2 **Compassionate (but firm)**. Your sense of compassion impressed me when you finally shut down the dentist. He'd been on a tirade about the misfit among us, an odd engineer full of conspiracy theories and shy on social skills. I'll call him Tim. We'd all rolled our eyes and commented, but the dentist kept doing it in poor Tim's presence. Tim had retreated from the table that day, but the dentist would not let the trash-talking go.

"Give it a rest." It was not a suggestion. You looked him in the eye and defied a response. Until then, you'd come across so amiably that the power edge in your voice silenced everyone at the table. Including the dentist.

Ah, I thought. *That was the plant manager talking. Good for you.* Hierarchy established.

Yet later that week, you could've been ten years old.

3 **Playful**. You bounced like a kid when someone suggested we walk into town for an ice cream. Your whole face lit up.

You bought a triple, of course, two scoops of chocolate and one of butter pecan. I noticed because as much as I love chocolate, I can't imagine enjoying butter pecan. We all watched, amused, on the ice cream shop porch to see if you could lick three scoops into submission before they succumbed to the tropical heat.

4 **Thoughtful**. On the way to the ice cream shop and back, you made a point of walking between the women and the road. We'd been warned about the crazy Caribbean drivers, and because you were big and thus readily seen, your positioning came off as chivalrous, not condescending. When several of us detoured into a bodega to explore, you bought that strange cookie, some tropical haystack, and offered a taste to everyone in the group. Your dadhood was showing, as well as your sweet tooth, but your unusual combination of gentle and firm was appealing.

5 **Capable**. The tropical diving that week was easily the best of my life, but you and I dove together only once. As the boat headed toward shore, you raised your voice. "Anyone want to dive off the dock this afternoon?"

"Me!" You were still a new diver, but I'd watched everyone in the group underwater, since lives can depend on knowing whom to trust. I'd seen enough to be comfortable with your skills.

A third diver joined us. At one point, I glanced back. You were nowhere to be seen. We were so close to shore that trouble seemed unlikely, but after a bit, I wrote on my slate, "Where's Tony?" You were the newbie, having completed fewer than two dozen dives. I felt responsible for you.

The other diver shrugged and turned back to the reef. I started to search, prepared to be annoyed if you'd gone in without alerting one of us. Then there you were, drifting up behind with your eyes on the reef, relaxed and unaware I'd even been looking.

For months afterward, that note stayed on my slate. By the time I had a reason to erase it, it had become a souvenir from the short days of our friendship before it transformed into destiny.

A Miracle in Process

Other than my admiration from afar, few sparks crackled between us in Dominica. My mind quenched them by habit. Even if you hadn't been taken, I was used to being treated like one of the guys, not a potential sweetheart. A date once called me "cute as a bug," which sounded patronizing but captured some truth: I'm more Dora the Explorer than Barbie. A male friend also suggested I was too threatening: too well-paid, too adventurous, too self-contained. I wouldn't pretend to be anything else, so I didn't often raise my own hopes for romance. My attraction to you was a bright falling star—a one-way delight that could only be fleeting.

But my dive buddy, Connie, noticed something I didn't. On the bus back to the Rousseau airport and our regular lives, she sat with you in the back row, where you splayed like the high-school jock you'd once been. I sat in the seat just ahead, swiveling frequently as we all laughed together.

I told you that you'd been our eye candy for the week. You blushed, which was exactly why I'd said it out loud. Just to tease you a bit.

That was when Connie struck. She insisted you and I exchange email addresses.

One of our older divers, she'd been the Group Mom all week. So we obeyed her, as awkward and shy as middle-schoolers. You complained that I knew more about you than you'd learned about me, so on a scrap of notebook paper, I wrote "For all things about Joni" with my email address. The unpaved road made my writing wobbly.

At the airport, four of us squished into a café booth to wait. Patti chattered nonstop at me while you talked to Connie.

"I wasn't going to talk about it this trip." The strain in your voice caught my attention. Connie, who had social services training, had drawn you into discussing your wife.

I bobble-headed at Patti while listening to you: Lynetta had stopped recognizing you long ago, stopped talking, stopped moving, stopped responding to tests of reflexes, stopped everything except blinking, slowly, at the ceiling. She was only a few degrees shy of a coma. Her body lingered, empty, still so young and physically strong that it might be another decade of hell for you both.

"It's cruel." You toyed with your Coke Light can, pinching its sides into angles. "Like I told my son, his mom was gone long ago. Why is she still here, dragging it out?"

Connie's words of comfort were interrupted when our flight was announced.

While we waited again at the gate, you sat on the end of my bench, the smile back on your face, and asked about walking trips I'd done in Europe.

What was happening here? My heart spoke: *It's a chance—be friends after this week.* Trying to ignore the first pangs of a crush, I wondered aloud if you'd be interested in being travel buddies. Anything more was impossible. The question still felt like a risk.

"Like to where?" You sounded surprised.

"Cinque Terre in Italy is next on my list." I described how much fun I'd had hiking in France and England. Your willingness to consider the idea seemed too good to be true. Small talk, I figured. Once we'd boarded our charter flight, I contented myself with stealing glances at you through the gap between the seats. That'd probably be the last we ever saw of each other.

But our group hung together when we reached the St. Maarten airport, where an invisible energy rose between you and me. A half-dozen of us waited for our next flight to Charlotte, and I realized abruptly you were in my physical space. Bending down toward me slightly, even as someone else spoke. Did you feel that strange electricity, too?

To see if you'd notice, I shifted closer. Encroaching for sure. You didn't shift away but edged even nearer. My whole body prickled with the charge.

Alas, our plane boarded, pulling us apart. In Charlotte, I spied you dashing past toward a conveyor, where bags had begun to pop out like Pez candies. They had to be collected for US Customs and then rechecked.

I called, "Are you going to make your flight to Nashville?"

Stopping short, you stepped over and leaned close. "Do you believe in miracles?"

By then, I felt the stirrings of one in process between us. "Yes."

"That'll be the only way I make it." Your red bag tumbled out and you hurried to get it.

"Good luck," I called.

Your flight took off without you, but I carried a glow home. My schoolgirl crush was hopeless, but it pleased me anyhow. I'd been single for more than a decade. The relationships that followed my gutting divorce had been fairly long-term but unsatisfying. I'd given up. My swoon for you was a total surprise—unexpected news that my romantic heart wasn't dead.

Once I got home, Facebook gave me another shock. Nearly every group photo that anyone posted showed us standing or splashing right next to each other. From the ice cream shop porch to candid shots on the boat, we were usually within inches, if sometimes back to back.

You later told me you'd noticed me early on. That you'd kicked yourself one night for retiring early and not taking a chance to stay up talking to me. That you'd encroached on *me* in the airport our last day. I wouldn't have believed you without this photographic proof. The snapshots seemed evidence of a magnetic attraction, one Connie had spied but that my practical nature had tried to keep secret from me.

But unseen forces aren't always unseen, and the Universe had already set fate in motion.

Bargains

Two bargains marked the start of our fairy-tale romance. A small group of divers witnessed the first, soon dubbed the International Pizza Incident.

Toward the end of our week in Dominica, you announced on the boat that you'd order a pizza for lunch if someone would split it with you. There were no immediate takers, so I agreed. After we docked, I ran up to change clothes. The kitchen worked on island time, so instead of pulling a T-shirt over my damp swimsuit, I took a quick shower before heading down.

It was not quick enough. When I got to the table, you'd eaten all but one nibbled half slice.

You turned red. "I didn't think you were coming. I thought you'd backed out." The others ribbed you, suggesting reparations: You should buy me a drink, an ice cream, an island.

"I owe you a pizza," you said.

Laughing, I scavenged a slice of pepperoni from the remaining crust and ate someone else's leftover salad while you remained at the table, marinating in embarrassment.

I didn't figure that debt would ever be paid. Besides, I felt repaid enough when the group walked to a fancier restaurant for our last dinner together. You took one end of the table, Lord of the Banquet that night, while I sat at your right hand to chat—treat enough. The table was surrounded with laughter, and the twinkle-lights strung all around us that night winked among tropical leaves, magical.

It turned out the magic had only begun. Barely a month after incurring your pizza debt to me, you did the honorable thing and repaid it. We shared a much tastier pizza on Maui, looking out over palm trees standing black against the sunset. That pizza marked only our second weekend together. Our first, two weeks after the trip where we'd met, had kicked off a whirlwind that swept us both away.

But the pizza wasn't the most important moment on Maui.

Oh, we shared many charmed moments in those seventy-two hours. Lying together on a chaise lounge under the stars, me trying to point out the Pleiades while you were more interested in bright spots on my body. Radiating smiles so broad, strangers offered to snap photos for us, even when our cameras remained in our pockets. Enjoying the sun on the nearly empty nude beach, our comfort with each other overcoming our shyness about our first experiences being publicly nude.

"You bring out a whole new side of me," you kept saying. "Tony 2.0. Asking me questions no one's ever asked, and now I'm doing things I've never seen myself doing."

We were simply making ourselves new together.

Even our misadventures that weekend were fun. Many men get cranky when something goes wrong. Your good humor kept going through every hardship, from our failed body-surfing and briefly losing your wallet to the urchin spines in your toe. That cheer was probably a byproduct of your Alzheimer's grief: You had valuable perspective on what's really important.

Maui matters most, though, for the bargain struck after our pizza. It announced itself in two parts. First, we were lying in your cozy B&B room that evening, our skin flushed with sun and surf and emotion. We snuggled under the lazy breeze of the fan, the only light from the blue LED on your portable speakers. Pandora Radio's Love

Songs station played all weekend long. The songs in that rotation are etched on my heart: IZ's "Somewhere Over the Rainbow." Jason Mraz's "I Won't Give Up." "Right Here Waiting," by Richard Marx. Aerosmith's "I Don't Want to Miss a Thing," which you later declared your favorite from that weekend. Its lyrics about limited time were about to take on more meaning.

Such a soundtrack makes it easier to be vulnerable, to risk being mushy. As we lay there, talking and tangled, we were. Your voice not much above a murmur, you sang, "Oceans apart, day after day. . . ." I listened, delighted. No man had ever sung to me before. Humming filled in for words you didn't know before you joined the chorus, "Wherever you go, whatever you do, I'll be right here waiting for you."

My right hand reached to your bare chest to thank you. To show you that you needn't wait. I was "right here" with you already despite the miles that usually separated us.

You started quaking beneath my fingers, holding in unexpected sobs. I tucked my face at your throat to surround you in comfort, assuming the emotion was more about Lynetta than me. We hadn't talked about her that day, but her specter was with us. The pain of her loss stiffened your face every time you got a text about her. Perhaps you even wished it were her there with you, laughing and active once more, and not me. Still, you trusted me enough to let that pent-up grief out. I was honored to be there to receive it.

But I misunderstood. Your hand covered mine and trapped it on your chest. "What did you just do there?" Your voice was tight with tears. "It felt like you reached in and poked at my heart. I felt you touch it. What was that?"

I wrapped you up tight and whispered that I loved you. I didn't add that I was grateful to be the one soothing your heart.

Now that I know your heart took you from me, that a flaw lurked in it that would stop it too soon, I see that moment more sharply. Did fate hiccup there? I want to believe we somehow bought you more time, that our coming together applied a temporary patch to that thumping engine in your chest. If you hadn't invited me to join you in Hawaii, where you visited your daughter before my arrival and went diving after I had to leave, would a heart attack have drowned you midway through your next dive? Perhaps you felt the awarding of bonus health points as the gamemaster, amused by our giddy love, extended your expiration date. *Ka-ching!*

That shudder of your heart was a preview for the bargain I made later that night.

After you fell asleep, I lay awake, too spellbound to close my eyes. That would remain true for months, for so many hours spent gazing in wonder at your profile, inches away in the dark. I was nearly certain I'd drowned on that fateful trip to Dominica and just couldn't remember the traumatic parts. The life I had lived in the past month, with you in it, was heaven. Either that or you were a dream, and I couldn't risk falling asleep because I might wake alone in my real world again. So I listened to Jeff Buckley's "Hallelujah" drifting from the speakers across the room.

Smiling up at the shadowy ceiling, I was struck by a bolt of awareness, a voice: *You can have this, but you will lose him.* I was going to have to suffer your death. The wave of knowing that crashed into me stretched beyond our ages. I'd just turned fifty-one. You had four years on me, but we both were as healthy as most people twenty years younger. I couldn't possibly put you through grieving another woman you loved, which meant that I had to be okay with you dying first. Statistically, you'd go first anyway, but this certainty was not about that. It felt like the Universe was making an offer: *Take it or leave it. There's no other choice.*

This intuition, so strong, made me cry. The first part, *You can have this*, was humbling. It wasn't language or a point of view my inner thoughts used. Yet one of your arms cradled me as you slept, and I felt unbelievably lucky, granted not just your love but a side order of grace.

I muffled my sniffles and took the deal as offered. And sang "Hallelujah" under my breath.

The Unseen

I t's fair to ask why I believed this intuition. College welcomed me as a budding scientist, after all, although two years of physics and its black-and-white answers drove me to the grays in the English department instead. I still think of myself as practical and grounded, but I'm open to experiences we can't explain. Why?

Blame my dead sister. My credulity started with her.

Jo Anna was my golden-haired toddler companion for less than two years before she died. I was three and a half when it happened. For years, my parents blamed dehydration from the flu, which had hit her a few days before her death. She seemed to be getting over it when she went into convulsions one morning. My dad was a young Air Force mechanic, and our family's rushed trip to the military hospital came too late. Only one Sensel child came home that day.

A few moments from my earliest years stick in my mind, including strobed images of that day and Jo Anna, but no memories of missing my sister are there. No recall of the hubbub or the relatives who arrived, no memories of wondering where she went. My parents' grief must have been shattering, too enormous to hide in a small duplex apartment, but my baby brain blocked it. She was just gone.

We didn't quite pretend that she'd never existed. Our photo albums, stashed away in the closet, contained only a handful of photos of her. My young parents had not owned a camera. We stopped by the cemetery on Easter two or three times, but like nearly everyone else in the

1960s, my family swaddled grief mostly in silence. My brother was born a year later. Jo Anna's name almost never came up.

It was an early initiation into a truth known by every child: the reality below the surface, the world of the Unseen. You told me enough about your mother's depression for me to know you experienced that shadow truth, too. Drugs and alcohol, mental illness, abusive treatment, affairs—plenty of families have unspoken secrets experienced by the very young. The idea of protecting kids from these realities is a joke that only teaches them to mistrust their parents—or themselves. During the 1960s and 1970s, every house I knew had a Skeleton Closet, some of them bursting. Jo Anna's death wasn't the only secret in my family, so I can't remember a time when I wasn't attuned to creepy feelings, intuition, and the certainty that Things Are Not What They Seem.

It didn't help that my grandmother's old house was haunted. A storage alcove in the stairwell to the second-floor bedrooms contained something hostile. It terrorized me when I was small—years before my mother shared the strange sightings she'd had as a child. As I grew older, I realized that whatever it was didn't have the power to escape its alcove or shove me back down the stairs. It wanted to, though. The space vibrated with malignant energy and resentment. As an adult I respected and avoided what my family came to call the Stair Ghost. Even my uncle, a science teacher, acknowledged its presence.

But I think the loss of my sister influenced me more. By the time I was seven or eight, I'd been gripped by a recurrent dream. Not quite a nightmare, it began with my walking in a long line of kids on a path that wound up a mountain. Some of the others were younger than me and some a bit older, not more than ten. Silent, we shared glances to encourage each other. Our feet crunched on the gritty path as we moved slowly upward.

I was nervous about what was to come. A clammy mist swirled

around, so we couldn't see far—only to a few kids ahead in the line. The higher we went, the denser the fog grew.

Abruptly, I'd reached the top. *My turn.* Empty space yawned to my right. A kindly old man hunkered on a stone at my left. The idea, I knew, was for me to jump off. As all the children ahead of me had.

The old man, at eye level, put a gentle hand on my arm. "Are you ready?"

I wanted to say yes but was too scared to answer. A question was stuck in my throat.

He seemed to realize that. "You're very lucky, you know."

Knowing he was right, I managed to ask, "But we'll have to die. Won't we?"

He nodded. "Yes."

His calm gave me courage. Knowing he wouldn't force me, I turned and jumped off—

—And each time I woke, aware that where I had landed was this life, this family. It wasn't in the dream that I had to die; it was here. That's the price of this privilege.

My parents were cautious about the TV we watched, and I never saw anything like this on Disney or Wild Kingdom. I can't imagine what prompted this dream if not Jo Anna's death. Whether a fragment of memory from before I was born, a whisper from the collective unconscious, or a direct message from her, it suggested she wasn't eternally lost but had only returned to that queue on the mountain.

The dream has stuck with me my entire life. It resonated in my teens when I learned about reincarnation and considered the idea that perhaps souls could choose whether to take on bodies. Maybe we don't have to jump, but it's worth it.

By the time you first kissed me, Tony, this dream hadn't crossed my mind in a while, but it's been in my thoughts a lot since you left. I realize now that no matter how painful or frightening they may be, our own deaths are not the biggest prices we pay. The real cost is facing the death of someone we love.

Regardless, that dream opened me to possibilities, to a numinous world beyond this one. The truths I knew in my heart might not be discussed, but that didn't mean I couldn't trust them. It was true of the alcoholics in my life, of a sister who'd vanished, of tensions at home, of the neighbor who beat his wife. The insights of this dream felt no different.

Maybe it's not a coincidence that I began writing stories at age seven, too. The *possible* drew me. If things are not what they seem— as they clearly weren't—what else might they be? My reading soon trended toward science fiction. Before long I was writing my own. It never occurred to me until after college that I could perhaps write a book, but then writing became my main play. A decade of screen-writing eventually morphed into five published novels for kids. It warmed my heart when you bothered to read them to share the possible worlds I'd invented.

Writers are known for imagination, but also for paying close attention to life. My openness to possibility was reinforced over time by other experiences that vibrated with meaning. One in particular I count as the epiphany of my life, not only because it was dramatic but because it merged spirituality with my understanding of physics in a way that made sense to me. My inner scientist found common ground with the mystic who developed after my sister's death. Fully awake one night in 1999, I had a vision that came out of nowhere. When it was over, I believed I'd glimpsed the nature of God.

Those words make me uncomfortable. I've deleted them twice. They sound both arrogant and delusional. Qualifying them with "or as much of it as my mind can grasp" doesn't help. But that label arrived with the insight and continues to arise whenever I think of that night.

The Nature of God

I'd had a great July day with people I loved. Full disclosure: Marijuana brownies had been consumed that afternoon, and although many hours had passed, they may have influenced the vision that followed.

In bed but lying awake, I was staring into the room's geometric shadows, reexperiencing the day with a glow. In writing this, I've realized this happened in the same liminal state as my bargain with the Universe, except that in Hawaii with you I'd been perfectly sober. Maybe that time of day sets my imagination wild. I prefer to think that's when the Divine talks to me, piercing through my usual defenses. No acid or ayahuasca necessary.

Comfortable and gazing at nothing, I began to feel a strange, buzzy sensation that I was watching myself—not in memories of the day but right there in bed. Inadvertently I'd performed some mental twist, glancing over my shoulder to catch myself spying on *me*. Part of my awareness was on the other side of some boundary, looking through at a smaller version of myself. The smaller me was the Joni of physical form, and the one who was watching was . . . something else. Something that wanted to be labeled my soul.

Startled wider awake, I stiffened, intrigued. Questions bubbled into my mind: *What is this window that, uh, we're looking through? How does it work?* Answers arose, sometimes as a voice or a sudden knowing, but mostly as a mental image. Mind, meet blown.

The first answer was that I was gazing across a sort of membrane, the barrier between the physical world and reality. It could be made more transparent, like a one-way mirror when the lights are turned off on the observer's side. Some people meditate to turn down the lights or use religious rituals to stretch the membrane thinner. Some people go to physical extremes, as in long-distance running or vision quests. Other people splash chemicals on it.

After such a full and obliging answer, I wondered if this was a hallucination. I'd had weird experiences before, mostly in dreams, but compared to those, this used Dolby and an LCD screen. And believe it or not, I try to be at least 5 percent skeptic. As a result I had a "wait—is this real?" moment.

Immediately came this answer, in exactly these words: *The pictures are real. It's the forms that are illusions.* I understood that this earthly life was a front; a more essential reality lay behind it. Behind the membrane, on the other side of the thin places in life.

Since my questions had been answered so promptly, I kept asking. "What *is* real, then? What exactly is there on that other side?"

My mind's eye can still see the answer: Streams of light that were consciousness, that merged and refracted the way white light can be split or unified by a prism. They wove and spiraled together like strands and coils of rope or a much more complicated DNA helix. I understood that this was the "coil" of life, every living thing with its own strand of light and all interconnected. Two strands might cross and then not meet again. Or a family, a circle of friends might entwine and move together, a cable in the overall braid. Those cables twist almost infinitely with others. They support one another where they intersect, and all the coils together make up the spiral of life. As light energy can behave both as a particle and a wave, consciousness is both individual and collective. That shared awareness of energies interacting is the foundation for experiences we find hard to explain, such as knowing when a distant loved one feels distress.

Every time I recall this, even twenty years later, awe rises within me at the inexpressible privilege of this epiphany. My heart was pounding. Adrenaline soured my stomach, too, but I was trying not to move because I didn't want it to stop. A sound or sensation or my own breath might drop the veil. Staring at the ceiling, my eyes grew dry as I tried not to blink. That, too, might end it. My attention was all inward on the mental image of this spiraling light, and my physical as well as emotional reactions left no room for me to doubt the authenticity of the experience.

I asked what this meant for the idea of reincarnation. The light streams showed me how they could refract like a rainbow into multiple colors and individuals. Little Orange would be separated from the whole for a while, incarnate over here in the narrow-band world of form. That was why people with near-death experiences saw white light. They're approaching, if not merging with, the rest of their strand.

Suddenly dubious—on guard against the dogma of my own childhood programming—I asked if this refracted light had anything to do with Noah's rainbow. Seeing a traditional rainbow, I heard, *That's a misunderstanding.* These words came with the absolute conviction that if rainbows mean anything beyond sunshine through rain, it isn't a promise. It's a reminder. We're all part of that greater braid, and we ought to be mindful of that unity and grateful for our interdependent lives. Gratitude matters.

More questions. More answers. I didn't always understand them. For instance, I asked about evil. Was it a discrete force? Dark stretches, like electrical shorts, appeared in the streams of light. I didn't know what to make of that. When I asked about fate, I saw a map and heard, *But you fill it in.* Then I saw stepping stones showing how seemingly unconnected parts of my life—my writing, my martial arts classes, certain people—had added up to who and where I was at the moment.

Later I thought, *Well, duh.* Looking back over a path, no matter how crooked, of course it leads to where you are now. But at the time my reaction was to laugh. *Ha! Of course! I see now how those things are connected, not random!* One example was how my martial arts classes had made me stronger, both physically and mentally, for the end of my marriage, which by then I secretly suspected was coming.

Eventually I asked about an afterlife. A skull and crossbones arose, and not because I'd asked about death. The symbol was a warning: Don't go there. Stop asking.

I asked if quantum physicists were going to figure out any of this. A tangible sense of inversion hit me, of things turned around backward, so strong I seemed to be falling from bed. To stabilize I had to press my palms to the mattress. I understood that dizzy sensation to mean that theoretical physics is looking in the wrong direction, outward at materials, rather than inward to consciousness. With major apologies to the late Stephen Hawking, we aren't finding ever smaller particles because they're there. They're there because we keep looking. Matter is a function of consciousness. It will therefore oblige us.

I asked if I might be allowed to do this again. Again, the skull and crossbones.

Okay, I get it. That's a "No."

Did I need to keep this experience a secret?

Don't talk about this with [one friend], who won't understand. That seemed weirdly specific but came with no other warning.

Then it felt like I was turning, or was turned, away. That was okay; by then I was exhausted. Drawing my gaze from that internal screen, I found the glowing light of my digital clock. More than three hours had passed.

It wasn't a dream. I got up to sit on the floor and scribble out notes by moonlight. They're still in my files. The writing is messy and scattered and includes, "pictures real, forms illusion," "rainbow = gratitude," and "the nature of God." In all caps in the middle, I wrote the last message I'd heard: "DO NOT DOUBT."

Crawling back into bed, I feared it would all be gone in the morning, my memory blank and my notes meaningless. On the contrary, the vision was burned into my brain. Over the next days and weeks, I saw reflections of that spiraling light all around me: the grain patterns in wood, the tangled branches of a tree, even a mother with her child in her arms jolted me, sometimes as inexplicable echoes of that brilliant coil.

I tried to share this revelation with people I trusted, but nobody knew how to respond to, "Guess what? I had a spiritual epiphany last night." I get it. I mean, how do you answer? "Uh . . . good?" No one seemed willing, let alone able, to talk about what it implied. When I couldn't make anyone understand why it felt like such a Big Deal, I stopped trying. Gradually I stopped thinking of the experience daily, but it was always easy to summon, a doorway I could walk past and glance into. It made me sensitive to spirals and other patterns—in nature, in flowing water, in clouds, and in life. Such patterns reassure me. There's a big picture here. Remembering keeps mundane trials in their place.

The entire experience calmed me and prepared me to make big changes. I'd been caught in a slow-motion crisis, questioning not only facets of my marriage but my career's apparent lack of social value and the decade I'd spent writing screenplays with award recognition but not much else to show for it. My vision helped me remember fate's current would win, so I might as well relax into it. At the same time, that impression of stepping stones encouraged me to adjust direction. Ocean swimmers can't fight a riptide, and some aspects of my life felt like equally futile tussles with fate. But just as swimmers can reach safety by changing direction and swimming at right angles to the current, I switched from writing screenplays to creating books for children. That shift would eventually result in my first published novel. Similarly, I began facing the issues in my marriage, which ended less than nine months later. That wasn't the result I might have hoped at the time, but it was the right one. It led to my much deeper love with you, Tony.

I didn't have the chance to share this vision with you. Since it happened more than a decade before we met, it wasn't near the top of my mind. But my bargain with the Universe came in on the same channel. That first vision, so affirming, had brought joy to my life and given me no reason to doubt it. A second brush with that higher perspective was welcome. Even if its message was hard.

Perhaps it's a conduit Jo Anna holds open. Perhaps it's only a dreaminess in me prompted by an early encounter with mortality that forced me, as a toddler, to imagine where my sister had gone. A Sunday-school heaven never appealed, but maybe I invented my own, so deeply buried I've experienced it later only as a glimpse from Beyond. Either way, I owe that perspective to her.

Her death certainly shaped me in other ways, too. I never felt invincible. I expected to follow her at any moment. As a result, I was shocked to reach thirty. Every year since has been bonus time.

Loss is baked into me, though. Until you left, I'd been lucky; my parents, my brother, and all my friends are still here. My bones know, however, that loved ones go away. My bargain was only a timely reminder to amplify my gratitude for you.

Another hidden gift that Jo Anna's loss gave me might be responsible for our romance. I didn't recognize this until my forties, when I started writing a novel about her, but I've always tried to live hard enough for both sisters. To experience new things. Take risks. Have adventures. If anyone bothers to buy me a gravestone, the inscription I'd like is a *Spinal Tap* movie reference: "She went to eleven." With the sound all the way up. That's why I travel, learned how to dive, and was drawn to an offbeat island, Dominica. Going to eleven was how I approached you, dancing to my intuition with the volume full blast. In that sense, Jo Anna not only goosed my intuition but got me to Hawaii with you in the first place.

Crazy

"I know this sounds crazy," I'd emailed you. Before Hawaii or bargains or pizza debts paid. Less than a week had gone by since we'd left Dominica, and I was suggesting I visit you the following weekend.

You first emailed me on June 3, 2013, the Monday after we'd pondered miracles at the airport. I'd resisted the desire to email you because I didn't want to come off as a stalker. Instead, I moved to Phase Two of Tactics for Stalkers, signing up for the next group dive trip you'd be on.

But wow! Here you were in my inbox. Even your P.S. made me smile: "It's kind of intimidating emailing a writer." You seemed so successful, so confident, that your uncertainty was endearing.

I was puzzled, though, by another line: "You promised 211 additional details by email. I'm listening. . . ." I ignored it until your next message said, "At least 207 more details to learn about you." So specific! Where had that number come from?

We untangled it over Skype later that week. On the scrap of paper with my email address, my scrawled "all things" looked to you like 211 things. We laughed about a new hotline in the 911 series—just call Joni-1-1! Secretly I celebrated: A simple mistake had made me sound intriguing. Fortune was favoring me. I took advantage of it by playing with you, sending emails pretending to be from an attorney, advising you why their client couldn't disclose more than a hundred things, or announcing that you'd won a prize in a sweepstakes but would have to dial my phone to collect.

Oh, and yeah, I saved all our emails. I knew I'd need them. At first I had to prove to myself I hadn't dreamed the whole thing. After Hawaii, once I knew you wouldn't grow old with me, I kept them to hear your voice in them once you were gone.

Your honesty in those emails caught me. The worst day of your life, you told me, had been making the tough decision to place Lynetta in a care home after the strain of tending her put you in the hospital. And yes, as you suspected, I'd Googled you, finding that old article in your local paper. I'd seen the photo of you kneeling alongside her wheelchair, love transparent on your face. I so respected that love and your loyalty to her and felt honored you would share such vulnerability with me.

So I was honest back, admitting that I had an eighth-grade crush on you but would be happy to only find a travel companion. (People who are married don't realize how much travel pricing is structured to penalize singles.) You responded that maybe you'd come visit Seattle, but Labor Day was the soonest you'd have time off work.

Amazed at your offer, I upped the ante. Did we have to wait until fall? I could come to your side of the world for a weekend.

I told myself I was being practical. It could be disastrous to go on an overseas trip with someone I barely knew. Compatibility in an airport after flights have been canceled might be more important than in a marriage! Being stuck with an awkward companion on my home turf sounded even more threatening; the freedom to leave beats potentially having to shove someone out. A visit to your home in Kentucky would help us make sure we could stand each other for more than two hours at a time and without the buffer of six or eight other divers. (Never mind that 2,448 miles across the country is a long way to go to meet for coffee.)

I couldn't believe it when you admitted, "No doubt if you were a little closer I'd want to ask you out, not sure if I could bring myself to actually ask or what we'd do, but I'd sure like to get to know you better. Heck, it's been a long time (at least thirty-eight years) since I've had such thoughts. So friends, travel buddies, or ???? works for me."

Boy, did my eyes fix on that ????.

You added, "If you lived closer I think we would have already spent some time together, so it's the distance that's crazy, not spending time together. (He said again and again.)"

"I like the way you think," I replied, pleased by the admission you, too, were convincing yourself. Our hearts and heads were struggling—but we both granted victory to the former.

I expected to find a hotel room not far from your house, but you let me know you had a guest room. "Besides, I just spent three hours cleaning it."

"No good cleaning should ever go to waste," I replied. *Ax-murderer?* only passed through my head as a reflex. I already knew you better than that, and having a black belt gives me a sense of security, false or otherwise. Besides, I'd seen bits of your house in our video calls. There may be ax murderers who tend indoor palms as healthy as yours, but I'd bet against it.

I bought plane tickets. And a summery dress. You could accuse me of calculation, I guess, but I wanted to make a good impression. The departure from my typical jeans and sweaters meant that five hours on a plane froze my ass off. That would've been great if it'd invoked actual ass-reduction powers, but it didn't. Only goosebumps. I warmed myself by staring out the window for the entire flight, imagining what might happen.

The Nashville airport was crowded. I spotted you before you saw me. Your height helped. You were scanning the crowd well over my head. Resisting the urge to wave, I could nearly touch you by the time you recognized me. Your expression as you took in the dress was worth every goosebump.

"I almost sneaked up on you!" I teased.

"I've only ever seen you in a rubber suit!" you protested. It wasn't true, but I was too busy wavering between a hug or a handshake to argue. You wrapped me in a hug. "Wow. You look great!"

Your house was a mansion; I'd have been out of my league even if you hadn't picked me up in a company Corvette. But you swapped your work clothes for sweats and made me a dinner of white lasagna, a nod to the Sicilian heritage of your last name, Alferio. Country music played in the background. You made me promise not to tell anyone that your satellite radio feed was sometimes tuned instead to the Love channel.

"Not good for my image at work," you explained with a sheepish grin.

Over white wine on your patio, we shared more secrets. Our guilty pleasures. Our Life's Most Embarrassing Moments. Your Catholic upbringing. My reasons for not being a Christian, despite a childhood that including mopping the floors of my family's Methodist church. So you wouldn't think I was an atheist, I explained my belief that all religions reflect our limited interpretation of fundamental truths—the consistent themes of love, gratitude, kindness, unity—filtered through, if not shredded by, politics and culture. I can still hear your firm, "I agree."

We moved on to my role in the implosion of my fifteen-year marriage and your struggles with Lynetta's illness, its effect on your adult kids, and how hard it had been to do anything but work as she sank beyond the reach of any voice, face, or touch.

I told you, from my heart, that if she'd loved you at all, she'd want you to be happy. I was not being selfish. I still think it's true. I admit that by then I was hoping for more, but I'd have gone home satisfied if we'd only cemented our status as travel buddies.

It didn't take you long to disabuse me of that pale goal. We took your dog for a walk under the streetlamps. We'd barely begun before you leaned over with a quick, awkward kiss. Startled, I let you take my hand and smiled into the dark.

Once we'd returned to your house, you said, "I want to improve on that kiss." Whew. "Improvement" was an understatement. Was this how it felt to be desired—by someone you hardly dared to imagine yourself with?

"We've got all weekend," I murmured, breathlessly racing to catch up with my heart. I've never had a one-night stand, or anything like it, in my life. Plus the anticipation was delicious.

With one more sweet kiss, we wished each other goodnight. My soul afire, I barely slept, but the next day was even better, ending on a restaurant patio lit by fireflies. Fireflies! Proof of magic in the world. They reminded me of the twinkle-lights our last night in Dominica. I wasn't sure the weekend could get more perfect.

Suffice it to say that it did, and I didn't spend another night in the guest room. Before the weekend was over, you'd invited me to join you for the Fourth of July in Hawaii as our earliest chance for reunion. One of your comments I'll always treasure was, "I didn't know it could be like this."

Me either, sweet. I was dazzled. By the middle of the next week, my friends were asking why I was glowing, and I was telling them I was madly in love. You must have been smiling more than you had in a while, too. In a text to me you revealed that the plant rumor mill was buzzing about a difference in you.

"Afterglow," you explained. You decided your poker face needed work.

Impression made? Check. I'd say the impact was mutual, but I don't think it was. You told me you felt like a teenager again. I hadn't *ever* had sensations like this. They drew me to write you emails like this:

Tony. I find myself just wanting to say your name, over and over again. To feel the vibrations of it in my chest and throat, as if that rumbly sensation was somehow you touching me—stroking me from inside, from my lungs to my lips, as if I'd inhaled you like a mist and could breathe you back out, summon you with your name like some kind of magic, and you'd appear before me to touch. The sound of it means so much more than your name, who you are, a way any old person could get your attention. It means hope and longing and every phone call we've ever had and every text you've sent me and the feel of your hands on my hot skin and the feel of them tangled in my own fingers as we walk on a beach or a trail or a random parking lot made beautiful and sublime by the mere fact of my hand in yours.

Feeling Fate

"**D**o you think we get what we deserve?"

Your voice muffled by a pillow, you asked me this question on my second trip to see you in Kentucky. This time we'd stayed in Nashville for a night as part of your successful campaign to convert me to country pop music. I was rubbing your back when you asked it.

Thinking about the bargain I'd made in Hawaii and wondering if you had made one of your own, I kept kneading. Probably you were feeling guilty about having a good time while Lynetta's existence had devolved to something most of us wouldn't count as life at all. How many times did you murmur, "I don't deserve this"?

The question reeked of your Catholic guilt. You absolutely deserved any joy you could find. Your loyalty and responsibility were among the things I loved about you. Lynetta certainly didn't deserve her illness, but no additional suffering could remedy that. You gave her the best care you could, and I hope now she's been able to thank you yourself. For those of us still on this side, the best evidence is that your son had to call an ambulance for you after fulltime work and twenty-four-hour caregiving dropped you. Terrified of losing you both, he helped convince you she needed a nursing home.

If anyone in our Nashville hotel room was undeserving, it was me. My first husband made me feel needed. You made me feel loved. You didn't need me—you were the most competent, capable man I've ever met, yet without the inflated ego that often follows success. I've never known a man I respected so much—an intoxicating combination of tender and strong. It was almost impossible to believe you'd bestowed your love on me. If I "deserved" you at all, it was only because we shared traits, like a sense of adventure, that I most admired in you.

In general, though, I think the question was wrong. "Do we get what we deserve?" assumes too many things we can't know. Most people deserve better than what they sometimes get, and everyone deserves love. If everyone felt a third of the love and joy we'd ignited, wars would end, and we could all work on fixing poverty instead.

Leaning into your back that afternoon, I debated: Should I answer the question you asked, argue with the assumptions behind it, or take this chance to bring up a Universe that makes bargains?

"I don't know about 'deserve,' but I kinda believe in fate," I replied. "Not for the details of life, but its outline. I think fate's like a river. It's going to take you somewhere. You can fight the current, you can get caught in an eddy, you can paddle hard to reach the left fork instead of the right. But sooner or later, the river's going to win. I do think the big things happen for a reason."

In a culture obsessed by free will, this is not a popular opinion, I know. More people put faith in chaos. But I'd learned just enough quantum physics to be dangerous, and materialist probabilities don't convince me. In particular, it seemed fate had helped us find each other, two needles on opposite sides of the haystack, when neither of us was looking for anything but colorful fish. A collapsing wavefunction, tides lapping in Dominica, the rushing river of fate, a murmur of intuition—it's all the same current, or so I suspect. Each exerts a pull on our lives, the gravity of the heart.

You didn't respond to my musings about fate, so I tried to simply give you more of the love you deserved. While ignoring the warning inside.

Terrible events could change someone's life overnight. That I knew. I hadn't realized windfalls could do the same thing. Before you, I'd been happy, if lonely. After our first weekend together, I walked through each day in wonder. My sense of the possible expanded immensely, along with my faith in love as a divine force. You completely changed my perspective on the Universe, which was so much more benevolent than I'd thought. The harsher blows of fate notwithstanding.

My view on fate has been influenced by stories of people who survived cancer or a car wreck only to have a tree fall on them three weeks later. Better, after you left, three different friends told me how they'd known on their first date, if not at first sight, that they'd met their future spouses. Their stories are full of unlikely conjunctions, including a collision with a tractor-trailer that, instead of killing her, nudged one friend into meeting her eventual husband. Another still has a diary from her teen years with the entry, "Tonight I met the man I'm going to marry."

That evening in Nashville, something more personal sharpened my faith. Two years before I met you, I was at a writers' event where the speaker conducted a guided meditation. The point was to see yourself in twenty years: Where would I be? What would I be doing? As I sat among friends in a college classroom, she directed us to visualize a future home, knock on the door, and watch our future selves open it so we could walk in to explore.

I played along, not surprised that the house springing to mind was a stone cottage in England. An extended visit had long been on my wish list. More shocking, the "older me" who opened the door wasn't alone. Behind her stood a shadowy, much larger male figure who completely derailed my meditation. He was not the smallish guy I was seeing at the time, not that I had illusions about *that* lasting twenty years. I hadn't expected anyone else there at all.

It's funny how something you're imagining can still surprise you, but you'll have to take my word that novelists are familiar with the sensation. I mentally gaped at that male companion: *Really? Who are you, Mr. Wishful Thinking?* In reply, I got the sense of the letter A.

Oh, right. I'd had previous encounters with this particular letter. In my crazy youth, I learned to perform hypnosis for past-life regressions. I'd had a regression myself on a lark, and the experience so stunned me that I wanted to bring it to others. Whether the past-life perceptions are authentic or not, they're great material for writers. During that week of training and practice, the letter A came up for me multiple times. I kept encountering a mental image or presence that seemed to be male but that, try as I might, I couldn't bring into focus. Frustrated, I played Jung: *Hmm, probably my own Animus.* When I later named the protagonist of a novel Aidan, I figured I was done with Mr. A.

Now, many years later, he'd appeared again in this meditation on my future. Recalling my previous A-man encounters, I dismissed him. The exercise was productive, however. It made me realize I didn't want to be doing the same things with my life in five years, let alone twenty. The meditation pushed me to end that relationship going nowhere.

Which led directly to my return to scuba diving, which I'd abandoned while seeing that non-swimming guy.

Which led directly to you, with your initials, A A, and a body much bigger than mine. We stood together in English stone doorways, too, didn't we? Even if my meditation timeline was wrong.

That experience, which shimmered like "knowing," might be nothing of the sort. There's no objective way to assess intuitions except in hindsight, where confirmation bias flourishes like mold on old cheese. Your initials didn't consciously affect anything I did. The correlation didn't even occur to me until that weekend in Nashville, where talking about fate surfaced those memories.

It made me smile to think some part of me had known all along. But it squeezed my heart, too. Being right once, though it had taken a long time to play out, made it harder to forget my intuition in Hawaii: *You can have this, but you will lose him.* The first clause of that bargain was coming true with more speed and force than I thought possible. We'd been together for less than two months—less than two weeks in person, given the mileage between us—but had blown past my shy crush. We'd begun planning our future. That abrupt gift of joy came as a proof of its corollary: pending loss.

But that was ridiculous, right? *Don't be dumb, Joni. You're making things up. Delusions are more common than quantum physics. That thing in Hawaii was simply knowing that men typically die first, prompted by a song about being over the rainbow.*

My pep talks weren't convincing. The premonition of loss I'd accepted in advance had packed too much emotional wallop. All I could do was hope it was wrong. *Please, let this be my imagination.*

Besides, death and loss lurk ahead for most everyone, don't they? Others seem to pretend it can't or won't happen. Heck, most people won't even make out a will. Somehow I missed Denial 101. Wishing for a remedial session, I tried to dismiss my premonition.

My belief in fate helped. Whatever was going to happen would happen, and there wasn't much I could do about it.

My foreboding didn't rise into my thoughts every day. Just on most days we were together. When we were apart, it was easy to focus instead on our next text, next email, next reunion. Whenever I had you in person, knowing that one of us soon had to leave reminded me of the greater loss I had foreseen.

But hey—maybe once we were living together, that fear, like my frequent flyer status, would vanish. I hoped so.

An Unexpected Opportunity

By the time we talked about fate in Nashville, its motion had been apparent for more than two weeks. It first appeared the morning after I agreed to my bargain. While we were still in Hawaii, in fact, fate's wheels began rumbling over a phone line.

We were lounging on a brick patio under the Maui sun while you took a call from an executive recruiter. You'd already turned him down twice, you told me, but you'd decided that morning to hear him out so he'd stop leaving messages daily. Island birds chattered in a tree overhead while he lobbied you through your Bluetooth earpiece.

He wanted you to interview for a job running a Navistar truck plant. What was left of the company once known as International Harvester, it made commercial trucks. While you asked about the plant's financial health and union relations, I worked nearby on my laptop. A few words filtered in through my focus, but I didn't eavesdrop intentionally because I thought you were simply getting him off your back. I was surprised to hear you schedule an interview at the plant.

After hanging up, you told me about what he'd said—and that I was partly responsible for your change of heart.

"I think for us it'd be better if I lived somewhere else," you explained. "Started fresh, maybe. Tony 2.0."

Startled but delighted, I asked where the plant was.

"Ohio. I'd be coming full circle." You'd been born near Cleveland, and the plant was in Springfield, only a few hours away from your siblings. "Besides, it'd be a chance to run my own plant." The job wasn't as sexy as working for Corvette, but it meant a promotion and greater control. The only other career goal you hadn't achieved was to live overseas with GM's international operations.

My first thought was that Ohio wasn't any harder to get to by plane than Kentucky. You'd been concerned about the hardships of a long-distance relationship, but so far they had barely posed an issue. We texted all day, talked every evening, and put every spare dime toward airfare. You had a plane ticket for Seattle later that month, as well as over Labor Day weekend. I would fly east again in August. Plus we'd arranged to room together for the diving trip in October I'd signed up for after seeing your name on the list. My amateur stalking had paid off! I counted the days before the next "Tony Day" until I could hail it as "the day after the day after tomorrow." We both called our reunions "Tony/Joni Days."

We'd also talked about Christmas together and had reservations for a February dive trip to Palau, our flights coordinated to meet on the way in Hawaii. Yours began in Kentucky and mine in Seattle, although when we made the flight reservations I'd said, barely joking, "Heck, Tony, if you keep me around that long I'll probably be camping on your front porch by then." A porch in Kentucky or one in Ohio. . . Unless Ohio didn't have fireflies, I wouldn't know the difference.

My second thought was to imagine moving to Ohio myself. After my first visit to you in Kentucky, I'd confessed to my parents about our weekend together.

Seeing how smitten her daughter was, Mom said, "Oh no, you're not going to move far away to Kentucky, are you?"

I sputtered more than replied, so she answered herself: "I guess, with his job, he probably can't move here, but you can work anywhere."

Yes, I could. My laptop had come with me to Hawaii for a conference call of my own that morning. Already, wherever you were felt like home.

"I've never been to Ohio," I told you. Business trips within ten miles of the airport didn't count. "But I can work anywhere with Internet service."

"You'd move to be with me?" You sounded surprised. "That doesn't seem fair. Maybe I should see if there's an opening at Boeing."

Astounded, my mind tried to wrap around that. You'd consider such a career shift an option? An airplane factory was still manufacturing, but you'd shown me your plant and answered endless questions. I had family members at Boeing and clients who'd formerly worked there. The cultures struck me as fundamentally different, and not in a way that recommended the latter.

You hesitated. "I'd have to think about what to do for Lynetta. Whether to try to move her. Or how."

We agreed to take it one step at a time. The Navistar interview came first.

You lit up again, even brighter. "Even if I don't want the job, I might be able to use it to get an international assignment from GM. They offered one a few years ago and I couldn't take it." That was a sacrifice you'd made to care for Lynetta. "You wouldn't be up for that, would you?"

"Absolutely! That'd be even better! What countries does GM have plants in?"

Germany, Thailand, China—we daydreamed a while. Once back home, I looked up Springfield online. A rust-belt city with its heyday in the late 1800s, its main enticements were the corn and soybean fields around it. But you would be there. I've never been a fan of the assumption that women ought to follow men, but I'd done it during college for far weaker reasons, and I couldn't wait to make every day a Tony/Joni day.

Looking back, the speed of subsequent events seems like one more confirmation of our limited time and a Universe pulling strings so we could enjoy it.

Destiny Accelerates

July 13—**Speed dating**. Though we were once more apart, our relationship deepened. The distance between us drove us to share feelings and fears with an intimacy that might have been lost if we'd lived in the same town. In a playful moment, I declared you my polar bear, both cuddly and fierce, tender and strong. You countered that I was your dove, or maybe an angel who'd come into your life. I had to bite back a laugh! Friends have characterized me as a wolf, a husky, and a squirrel. While dove seemed a long way in a softer direction, I loved what it said of your tenderness toward me.

Even better, you invoked the word "soulmate," admitting that was a bold thing to say but remarking how uncanny and destined it felt. That confirmed my own sense of a spiritual connection. Between us we probably spent three hours a day pouring out our hearts in long emails and phone calls. Those insights and admissions enriched our times together. As I noted midmonth, "A couple of hours or a weekend with you can seem as full as years and decades of life." The next four months proved it.

July 24—Career swerve. You were offered the job and a substantial pay raise. GM couldn't make a better—or international—offer. Your career took a hard right.

Although I teased you by saying, "Most of the executives I've known were jerks," I was excited for you. The role would give you more authority and new challenges. Your favorite shirts—shocking yellow, bright red, lime green—suggested you bucked the boring norms of business, but I knew enough about leadership to suspect you would make an outstanding top dog.

Tony 2.0 launched. Ohio gleamed in my future.

August 8—Zero to sixty. On my second trip to Kentucky, the one that started in Nashville, I met your favorite work friends when they celebrated your retirement from GM. Two pulled me aside to whisper how pleased they were for us and how much you deserved a new happiness.

They also razzed you about finagling a yellow pre-production Corvette to get us from Point A to Point B for the weekend. It felt like a spy car—great fun! As a test build not yet on the market, it drew men and boys like fruit flies each time we parked: "Hey, is that the new model?" "Can I touch it?" "How fast can it go?" You invited a few enthusiasts to sit behind the wheel, but I was more privileged—I got to drive it. On a back road we tested its zero-to-sixty acceleration, nearly a match for our own as we packed up your house for your move to Ohio and plotted for me to join you the following spring.

August 15—Trucking along. My next visit immersed me in Springfield, where you'd begun your new job. While you worked, I house-hunted for you—and for us, an idea I was still getting used to. In the meantime, the company put you up in a B&B cabin built on stilts like a treehouse, with a pine-plank ceiling and rustic log bedframe. It overlooked a field filled with fireflies—galaxies of them!— blinking the buggy Morse code of my love.

We both had to work that Thursday and Friday, and I rose with you those mornings at five o'clock, a feat for a night owl like me. You assured me I didn't need to, but the Aerosmith tune you'd sung for me in Hawaii had it right: I didn't want to sleep through a moment.

I'd rather drive you to the plant and pick you up at lunchtime. Before long the plant sign prompted a rush of emotion in me: joy, gratitude, wonder. The yellow Corvette had been fun, but my heart still surges at that orange International logo on the grille of a truck. I can spot them from two blocks away. That orange diamond brands the huge risk you took to create a new life that made room for me.

August 27—Highway speeds. After I narrowed the options to three Springfield houses, you chose the one with the most fireflies. Yay!

By then, the following spring sounded too far away. You lobbied to hasten my move, planned as a road trip with a small U-Haul trailer.

"How about January?" you said. I had a February plane ticket that left from Seattle, but you were ready to write off such minor objections.

"Won't the roads in states like South Dakota be awful?" I worried. "The pass in Montana will be for sure." The trailer would tax my aging Honda even without snow, and I worried about ice closing highways. But a longer route through the warmer Southwest would take more days than you could leave work.

"Okay," you replied. "Let's do it sooner. I'll have the keys to the house by October fourteenth."

We settled on the earliest practical date and broke the news to my parents on Labor Day, when they met you. My mother had gotten the state I was moving to wrong, but otherwise she'd called the results of this race from the start. She must've seen it in my face after our very first weekend. Now she'd be losing her daughter on November 6, five months after your first email to me.

Fate's River in Flood

There's a strange disconnect between the head and the heart. Our minds like certainty. Our hearts, maybe not—or at least they know what they want, unknown outcomes be damned. Starting with the first time I'd boarded a plane to Kentucky, my head had *no idea* what would happen. My heart only urged me forward, to dismiss reason and fly. The blank destination was part of the charm.

That delight continued as I rented a trailer and began loading it with essential possessions. What would a Midwestern winter be like? Which of my clients would still hire me? Would our two male dogs become friends or cage fighters? My heart couldn't encompass our love faltering, but there were so many things my head couldn't know. Weirdly, that ignorance made it more fun.

Before the thrill of that contrast between heart and head, I hadn't realized how uncertainty had seeped out of my life. Travel and adventures had not been enough. Maybe that was because, although I'd let my whims lead me, my head did the planning and stayed in control. Now that you and I had abandoned safety, if not common sense, infinite possibilities had opened for us. Okay, perhaps I would eventually lose you. In the meantime, our future was boundless. Our hearts had blown us beyond the horizon, and impossible things had begun to happen. I was moving to Ohio, for crying out loud, a state I had never given a second thought. Every day looked exciting, extraordinary. It's corny, but I felt reborn.

The largest of my practical worries was the response from your kids. You'd been catching flak from our first weekend together, not only from your daughter but from her in-laws, who apparently saw a photo of us on Facebook, declared you were shaming the family, and made sure that opinion reached you through mutual friends. Your son was more equivocal, probably because he'd been with you throughout his mother's decline. Your daughter, who was nearly thirty and might have had more compassion for you, had spent much of her mother's illness three time zones away in the great State of Denial. My arrival on the scene forced her to confront the truth. She seemed to choose fury as less painful than grief.

I didn't want to cause strife in your family. In our early days, when I could still imagine slowing, if not backing away, I said so. "It'll only cause a problem for her, and only if she makes it one," you told me. But your kids knew all the buttons to activate your indulgence, and she had a habit of calling unannounced to berate you, so I couldn't help but overhear a few of the volleys. Vanishing to another room wasn't always an option.

Your resistance to her made me feel championed, though. When you asked her how many years you had to be alone until you could move on with your life, you got a "More!" I could hear six feet away. She followed that up with "Until I tell you!" That seemed to trigger your inner union negotiator. "I'm not asking your permission," you told her firmly. That wasn't the first or last time she hung up on you.

The last battle in her war began in a call that woke us one morning at two thirty. Her shrieking on the other end was louder than you were—until your patience broke and you yelled. That shocked me too much for me to recall what you said, but you hung up this time, slamming your cell phone on the dresser afterward. The screen's survival should have been submitted to the Vatican's Miracle Committee. Though well-deserved, your anger made me glad it had never been directed at me. You'd told me about a work mentor long in your past who'd helped you overcome a bad temper, but I hadn't been able to imagine it until then. Your anger did its job, though. Your daughter's complaints fell to an occasional grumble, and eventually she announced that one of her coworkers, perhaps in self-defense, had convinced her that "everyone needs a companion." That word choice made me feel more like an elderly aunt than a sweetheart, but the coworker still earned my gratitude. The frequency of contentious phone calls was one uncertainty I didn't mind losing.

Once that friction eased, all our unknowns looked exciting. Yet nightmares descended on me for the whole endless week before we'd planned to begin living together. I was stuck in Honduras diving without you, since your new job had nixed the vacation you'd planned, and you'd insisted I go with the group regardless. The diving provided fishy distractions, but weak phone and Wi-Fi service cut us off more than usual. My nights were filled with floods and disasters and flashbacks to my painful divorce, with its sense of betrayal, rejection, and failure. I kept gasping awake in my tropical room, glad to find its unfamiliar shadows dry and not dripping. Pipes hadn't burst, waves weren't rolling through, walls were not cracking and washing away.

These nightmares left me puzzled as well as restless. Happier than I'd ever been—while awake—I couldn't wait to see you and start our new life together. Even sorting and packing stuff to bring had been fun. Why wasn't my subconscious on board?

It wasn't the ocean I was diving in daily. Vivid dreams have always caught my attention, and threatening water is, for me, a subconscious shorthand I deciphered a long time ago. It stands for crushing emotion.

Belatedly I recognized why my dreams had gone sour. I was scared. Not for any practical, head-centered reason; I was keeping my house, which we planned to return to once you retired. It gave me an escape hatch if our love somehow curdled and I had to flee back to my nest.

No, I was afraid of disappointment or loss. It had been a long time since I'd had so much to lose. After my divorce, I'd become self-contained, with a new home, new habits, and largely new friends. But the upheaval had plunged me into years of depression, and that was *after* my married life had turned into a mudflat. Oh, how much further I had to fall now!

An email conversation I had during the first fireworks of our relationship came back to mind. Connie, who made sure you and I exchanged contact information as we left Dominica, had let me gush to her about how happy I was. She deserved thanks! Her reply had contained a few puzzling lines: "I think you know that part of our 'mission' here is to experience fear in all forms, and overcome it with love and light. So I hereby dub you 'Fear-Buster Joni.'"

When I got that email, I wondered what made her think I was scared or had any reason to be. Now I knew. That made twice she'd seen my heart's path before I did.

To soothe the gnawing fear, I shared it with you, though email was the only way we could connect. "What if all the emotions between us, some anger eventually or frustration or hurt feelings or loss, are as intense as the love is?" I asked you. "Eek. Is that what you meant in a text not long ago about the intensity being scary?"

You reassured me you were scared too, afraid you'd hurt me or that our emotional adrenaline might wane. Yet neither of us wanted to reconsider. At my confession of fear, you reflected my own words back: "It wasn't that long ago when my Dove/Guardian Angel told me 'that she would rather have experienced our love than to never have realized it existed, even if it was for a short period of time.' I concur with that statement with my whole heart and being."

In fact, I said that more than once. From our earliest days, I charged friends with reminding me if it all crashed and burned. An email I sent you when we'd been together six weeks said, "The intensity of what I feel for you is probably going to burn out our poor bodies like rocket fuel sooner rather than later, and it will still be more than completely worth it." The sentiment is still true. That's partly why I'm revisiting all this with you. I need the reminder, again and again. My heart never doubted the course we had set, and I wasn't going to trust it that far and then stop, not when it had led me to joys I'd never known. But it wasn't wrong to be terrified, either. It knew what was coming on the other side of our peaks—a chasm made deeper by the heights we soared to. Our transit of heaven took more than three years, but my unease in Honduras feels now like a glimpse forward through time.

Maybe such views are beyond time and space. I envision a clear drinking glass, filled with the waters of the collective unconscious. Psychologists view the collective unconscious as a cache of instincts, symbols, and patterns, but it could also be the life force itself, our shared link to the Divine and each other. The drinking glass in my example holds all that unites us. Our conscious minds march like ants on the surface as if it were flat. We're mostly unaware of its contents. While we're awake, we see only forward or back. Falling asleep, we sink into that water, where archetypes, like amoebae, swim through our dreams. From that perspective, perhaps we can peer through the water, glimpsing the future we've yet to reach on the surface. Big changes refract through our subconscious minds.

In Honduras my dreams were apprehension of loss, of the devastating grief I'm struggling with now. Ignoring the knowledge I would lose you hadn't worked. It only leaked into my dreams. So I focused instead on cherishing you. On feeling the dread and loving you anyway, grateful for the gift fate had granted. The definition of courage applied. I dialed up the volume on not missing a thing.

PART 3

TOGETHER

Father Time
Stomps on the Gas

Leave now

← Turn left onto State Route 410 E

↑ Merge onto I-90 East

↑ Continue 2,363 miles

Arrive: five days later

O n November 6, you drove me, my car, my dog, and my U-Haul over the Cascade Mountains toward Ohio. We hit enough snow to be glad we hadn't delayed another week. Central Montana was treacherous, though. Damn, that state is empty. I eyed the limp fuel gauge for about fifty miles, saved from committing a back-seat-driver offense by the lack of any gas station where we could stop. You noticed, too, before I said anything. The sky gleamed blue as the car's amber fuel light lit.

I scanned electronic and old-fashioned paper maps for an exit. An exit sign loomed, raising our hopes—followed fifty yards later by a "No Services" notice. At least we didn't waste gas searching. This Duet of Dashed Hopes repeated twice more. The roads served by these exits seemed to go nowhere, maybe only to far-off ranches. No truckers or other cars passed. The brown, wrinkled land refused to give hope that maybe, if the car sputtered to the side of the road, we could hike to a farmhouse and buy a half-gallon of siphoned gas. The few loafing sheds between us and the horizon were empty even of cows.

A lone gas station at the end of a sole-purpose exit appeared in the nick of time, barely. Its deserted pumps made it feel like a Twilight Zone outpost. I'm not sure it wasn't. No other car or building could be seen, nothing went past on the highway while we pumped, nobody inside the office seemed to move or look out. A Hollywood tumbleweed would have been right at home. As we pulled back onto the highway, the tank again full, I used your meticulous gas and mileage records to calculate how close we'd come. We'd rolled into that station with four spare tablespoons of gas.

The Universe seemed to be looking out for us, aware we didn't have an hour to waste being stranded. Father Time put the pedal down in other ways, too, clearing the road for our racing hearts.

Fragile

You once mentioned you'd told Lynetta about me during a regular bedside visit to her. Your transparency didn't surprise me. What I didn't expect was your gallows humor as you added, "She didn't say much about it, so I guess it's okay." By then I'd seen for myself how far past understanding or caring she was. Yet she was still your wife, if only in name, a phantom who joined us in small moments and large. I know your grief and loyalty weren't easy to juggle with the need to keep living yourself.

When you took your new job, the experts who cared for Lynetta advised you that she'd best stay where she was. She didn't know the difference between one room, one facility, one state and another, but transit would be too hard on her body. Too stressful.

I think we both were relieved. It'd be harder to monitor her care and condition, but we'd be only five hours away. You were already paying a family friend, a social work student, to visit daily and ensure her comfort when you couldn't stop by, and that could continue. Your son also began to visit his mother more often, which helped him better come to terms with his grief.

I'm rationalizing that decision, aren't I? Soothing not only your guilt, but mine. I helped you unpack after your move from Kentucky, tackling cartons marked "kitchen" while you set up your garage. Each bowl and spice jar that emerged from the boxes had a story and Lynetta's fingerprints on them. A married lifetime of memories glowed from the silver and glass—wedding china. Fish platters. Souvenir saltshakers. The process provoked tangled feelings in me. No wonder you stayed in the garage, sorting tools, while I unwrapped and stowed these domestic reminders, this residue of one life borne into the next. I tried to honor each teacup, each candlestick holder, even dishes I found atrociously ugly and gadgets that had clearly never been used. What befell her is tragic. And benefited me.

I still can't believe you didn't visibly react when you learned my birthday was the day after hers. I only figured it out while shelving your books, when I found her birth date listed in your family Bible. The odds are one in 365, I suppose, give or take a leap year or two. The coincidence still raises the hairs on my neck.

I feel incredibly grateful to her. She certainly didn't do it intentionally, but from my side of our timeline, it seemed as though once she lost the ability to love you, she turned you over to me.

My sense of her generosity isn't unfounded. In a final post to the online journal where you'd shared her condition with friends, you mentioned that before her diagnosis, she'd worked with a physical therapy patient whose dementia had stolen his ability to communicate. At the time, she'd told you, "If I ever get to that point, it's time for you to move on. Put me in a home and don't come back." Shocked, you took years to realize what she'd learned—that the beloved is gone long before the body. You refused to walk away so bluntly, but at last you'd understood and accepted her point.

Maybe her spirit reached the Other Side before her body, which cruelly lingered for so many years. She might've been nudging you from Beyond. Heck, my warning that I couldn't keep you may have been a message from her. I'm sure she was waiting for you when you died. Her body gave up fewer than six months before yours did.

We didn't know that when you moved to Ohio, of course. When I admired the pattern on your wedding china, you surprised me by suggesting we get rid of it—give heirlooms to your kids and donate most of the cabinet's other contents to Goodwill.

"We never used it anyway," you grumbled, in tones that made me wonder if grief wasn't the only emotion involved. "Or we can use it if you want," you added, but your desire to move away from the past sounded louder.

I kept a teacup and saucer on the counter for a while, and not only because it was pretty. I needed to honor the bride who'd originally unwrapped it. After I'd moved in too, I steeped tea in that cup once or twice. But I'm a mug girl at heart, so the china eventually went back in the cabinet. When your kids took most of its contents eighteen months later, it pleased me. We wouldn't have room for them later, but consigning those heirlooms to Goodwill would have hurt.

Even our everyday dishes murmured of the bonds between us, practical ties if not legal or spiritual ones. When I slipped breakfast eggs onto one of your plates, slid your oatmeal bowl into the microwave for you, or chose one of "your" forks over "mine" for my lunch, I thought of the residue of your first life on them, their place in the meals we now shared together, and how they connected all three of us—you to her, you to me, and me through you to her.

Both those cheery place settings and the idle teacups marked time. They may have added to an undercurrent of loss, like the daily texts you received telling you of her status, that kept me ever mindful of our precious love. Nearly every moment amid the chores and laughter in our new home, a sense of fragility lurked under the surface.

Trying to Tell You

Several times I tried to tell you that I knew I would lose you, usually as we slowly relaxed into bed. The energy that built up there between us often felt like it shot sparks from my fingertips. Overwhelming, it threatened to burst out beyond us. Thank you for making it so clear you felt it, too.

But coming down from that high to sleep usually took longer for me than for you. So we started every one of our nights together with you holding me close to your chest. Those moments were my favorite part of every day, even during our most exotic adventures. From our double sleeping bag in our backpacking tent to that time we slept on the cold tile of the JFK airport, finishing the day nestled into your chest was pure joy. I admit sometimes I slipped back out of bed for lotion or lip gloss or any thin excuse simply for the chance to settle back once more into your embrace. Anything dreadful that happened, even the time we stupidly smashed our new camper, could be healed by my cheek on your skin, the *thump-thump* of your heart under my ear. That engine sounded deceptively powerful and perpetual. Until it became as familiar as my own, your heartbeat, an audible proof you were real, often reminded me of that night in Hawaii.

"I don't know if I should say this," I whispered once into your chest. We were living together by then, sharing every hour outside of work. Our toothbrushes shared the same holder, our dirty socks snuggled in the same laundry basket. I had your medicines in my purse and you'd put my name on your bank account. In this intimacy, my secret had been weighing on me.

My throat clogged. "I know . . . how hard it has been for you with Lynetta." I thought I did, anyway. I know better now. "I can't let you go through that again. And I won't."

Too teary by then, I couldn't form the next words: that I knew you'd go first and accepted the grief. Your love was worth it by far. I wanted you to know that. And I would do anything to spare you more pain.

"Oh, hon." You squeezed me tighter. But I was glad to hear gratitude in your voice, not dismissal. Not, *What makes you think you can control anything?* which was probably closer to what you were thinking. And more realistic for the world we live in, which honors the sharp voice of reason over the murmurs of the heart.

Sorry I'd brought it up without expressing either my love or your worth, I sniffed back tears. The gloom in our bedroom accused me, waiting for me to meet an obligation, to acknowledge the divine gift I'd received. While I searched for new words to explain my foreboding, your breathing shifted. You'd slid into sleep.

I'd dug at the splinter without getting it out, but I didn't try to mention my premonition again. I told myself I was being a goose, injecting doom and fear where it wasn't needed. Or helpful. Live for now, right? It wouldn't change what we did. You couldn't simply agree not to die. Musing, I questioned my motives. Had I inherited the martyr gene in my family? Why did I even want to tell you?

Because it felt like a secret I was keeping from you. A blotch in the deepest intimacy I've ever known, one that sometimes made it hard to maintain eye contact with you. Your dark, steady gaze could touch something in me even more intimate than the places on our bodies we didn't share with anyone else.

Maybe I should have tried harder. Revealing a secret can nullify it; if we had talked about my bargain, could we have drained its power?

But I have no illusion of control in our lives. Since I'd told you my views on fate, and you frequently accused me of reading your mind, would it simply have shadowed our love or your life? You already knew how much you meant to me.

No. Exposing my dread wouldn't increase our love. Gratitude, mindfulness, paying attention—those seemed a better way to embrace it. Loving to eleven now, today, while we could.

Rather than sharing this one burden, I wrapped my heart more snugly around you. Perhaps if I held tight enough, I could keep you.

Driving Your Truck

Though you drove my Element for most of the road trip that put me in your arms every night, we went nearly everywhere else in the cab of your GMC truck. One day while headed toward IKEA to buy a couch, we passed a massive church steeple that must've triggered a memory. You told me about a guy you once worked with who also served as a pastor in his church.

"He told some of us at the plant what he preached to his flock," you said. "Making love isn't just something that only happens in bed. It can be how you spend all the time in between. How you treat each other in the everyday stuff. Opening doors. Getting coffee. Putting the cap on the toothpaste." You patted my leg, a demonstration. "I've always liked that idea."

"I love it!" There's a dog-training approach I've used with success that considers every interaction a training moment, a message to the dog about the relationship. Your definition of lovemaking was a more romantic version. No wonder you insisted on hauling my luggage, putting your jacket around me when I broke out in goosebumps, and bringing me mugs of tea I didn't expect. Everything we did for each other could be making love.

Sign me up!

Our new home was easy to view through love-tinted glasses. Its Midwestern porch columns made me feel like we lived in a bank, but drawing on your Italian last name, I thought of it as First Alferio

National and adored every moment we spent there. Dirty laundry tugged my heartstrings, my underwear tangled with yours. That turned it from a chore to a service—and foreplay. Cooking dinners together, heating your oatmeal at dawn while you showered, even your solution when the furnace broke down—a fan propped in the oven, your "redneck heater"—became ways to make love.

Buying chocolate did, too. I didn't realize until we were living together that you were as much of a chocolate junkie as I was. Your executive assistant revealed she kept a bowl on her desk stocked with snack-sized chocolate bars exclusively for you. Once your cover was blown, we could share our addiction. Our favorite fix became dark chocolate bars bought on the road. Once we were driving again, I'd feed squares to you, your mouth open comically wide to receive them. Chocolate is known as "the love drug" anyhow, and sharing it that way became a small way to make love when highway safety prevented anything else—and never mind your country music favorite, "All Over the Road."

Maybe such a lens imparts meaning to things that would otherwise go unremarked, but the Universe seemed to engage in conversations with us. You'd been clear from the start, for instance, that you liked country music. I was a card-carrying member of the Anti-Twangy-Music Brigade, but your love for today's country pop, so much more like rock, made me reconsider. One day before we'd found our Springfield home, I was working in your rented treehouse to the sound of the XM radio you played twenty-four hours a day. I simply hadn't bothered to change the station. A song came on that caught my notice. After Googling the lyrics, I began to pay more attention.

Your music grew on me quickly because its themes and attitudes were so optimistic compared to my previous diet of blues, old rock, and alternative pop. It's mostly about love and connection to each other, our pasts, and nature. And beer. Country music has way too much attachment to booze, and we laughed about the obligatory references to a truck or tractor, but the genre's heart won me over. It became our special soundtrack.

The song that first made me listen was Lee Brice's hit, "I Drive Your Truck." I had just begun to drive yours. It was the first country song I bought for my phone, and we had a good reason to talk tenderly about it. Your nephew had been killed in the Middle East a few years before, and the song recounts the grief of a soldier's surviving brother. It also made me imagine slightly different losses. When I dropped you at the airport for your rare business trips, I had to take care going home not to cry or hyperventilate. Would I someday drive your truck without you? Ohio highways, eerily empty by Seattle standards, know "traffic" only as an adjective that modifies "ticket," but I did want to stay on the road. Once home, I couldn't bear to look at your empty truck until it was time to pick you up again, safe.

But the song struck me as joyous, too, because it evoked hundreds of moments driving in your truck together, from camping trips to quick jaunts to the store.

"Scoot on over here, baby," you'd say, though I was already tucked alongside you in the middle, not in the passenger seat. Attached at the hip all but literally. Your hand frequently rested on my leg, or vice versa. Sometimes you'd sing me a few lines of a song as it played on the radio. "I hold on," or "You be my honeysuckle, I'll be your honeybee." Your singing to me, off-tune as it was, flooded my heart almost as much as snuggling against you each night.

Brice opened our first concert in Cincinnati, where I teared up at another of his songs, "Love Like Crazy."

"You okay?" you asked when you noticed. "What's wrong, hon?"

You couldn't understand why such a happy song made me cry. Because I loved you like crazy, but the couple in the lyrics got fifty-eight years, and no way were we getting that much. It touched me for the same reason a few other tunes did: "Don't Want to Miss a

Thing," or "God Gave Me You," or Jana Kramer's song called, "I Got the Boy." The next words in the chorus are "she got the man," and Lynetta came to my mind each time it played. Music had never before narrated my life.

When "I Drive Your Truck" first caught my attention, I related most to what it said about adopting a loved one's favorite possessions. Now, as I feared, its grief has caught up with me, too. I drive *your* truck, without you ever in it. The radio stays tuned to the news stations, though. I can't get through a whole country song without tears. That first one of ours, painful as it is, runs in my head whenever I drive your truck. It reminds me the Universe never misled me about what I'd agreed to when I took the deal I was offered.

Clockwork

Your fourth email to me, less than a week back from Dominica, had ended with the line, "One thing I have learned is that time doesn't stop for anyone." It wouldn't go silently, either. Ignoring my premonition was impossible. The *tick-ticking* wouldn't shut up. Even once we'd stopped scheduling cross-country flights and counting the days before a reunion, time was always, always on my mind, thanks to a Universe that kept sending reminders:

- Your first Christmas gift to me, which you insisted I open two months early while we stood in the kitchen we soon would be sharing. The box, about right for jewelry, alarmed me, though I tried not to show it. You couldn't have missed my indifference to bling; the new dive flashlight you'd handed me, unwrapped, a few days before was the kind of shiny object that reflected our relationship better. Regardless, why did I need this Christmas gift early?

  Overanalysis gave way to relief and delight when I opened the box to find a shimmering watch. Its silver and pearl, so much like the moon, spoke more truly of our love than a diamond. For a moment I wondered what prompted that choice. But your timing and taste were both perfect—the watch gave me a special way to track the hours of our last separation before we'd be living together.

- Your last Christmas gift to me, a second watch, sunny yellow—
  as if I didn't treasure the first one and wear it daily.

- The more than half-dozen clocks you installed in our house, in
  every room, on the patio, in the garage, on your boat. Bemused
  by your affection for them, I watched you arrange them and
  keep them in sync. The one that projected red digits on our
  bedroom ceiling gave you such satisfaction that we soon owned
  a second. We could wake at any hour and without lifting our
  heads blearily confirm we had more time to sleep. More time,
  period.

- Another country song you called one of your favorites, which I
  attributed mostly to the loss of your wife: "Live Like You Were
  Dying."

- The last movie we saw together, *The Arrival*, in which the heroine learns to see beyond linear time to the sad end of her own
  love story before it begins.

So many of those reminders were driven by you that I have to assume
you felt the time pressure, too, some instinct about the hour of
your own expiration. But the prophetic instinct that most strikes
me as eerie concerns the Shutterfly book I put together for our first
Christmas and filled with photos from our first joyous six months. I
couldn't resist an impulse to buy more than one copy. I changed the
quantity in the online cart a couple of times before giving in and
ordering two.

Neither of them was given away. The first I shared with you and
anyone else I could pin down long enough. The second copy I kept for
myself, writing in my early impressions of you and comments others
had made about us. I inserted the lovely cards you'd given me, your
handwritten "I love you" Post-its, and the US map we'd drawn and
tried to label together as a game. Even after we'd driven through ten

or twelve of those states, your confusion about the western US was exceeded only by my rearrangement of the I states and the Mid-South. When we pooled our massive intellects to fix it, our Geography of Blobs still left off three or four states. But who needs Connecticut and Delaware, really? I've never laughed so hard as I did that evening, so I squeezed that map's giggles into my Tony scrapbook.

To top it off, during our first winter in Springfield, you pulled a shred of paper from your wallet and said, "Remember this?"

I didn't recognize it until it was in my fingers. "Ah!" The scrap with my email address and our "211 things," you'd carried it with you every day since. Sentimental. And close to your body.

I asked if I could keep it, knowing exactly where I wanted to put it. "Sure."

That scrap went into my memory book too, which I shuffled between folders on my desk. I didn't want to explain that copy if you saw it.

Twice, while home alone, I pulled out that book, stood with its slight weight in my hands, and felt guilty about keeping it hidden. We didn't have secrets. The only thing between its pages we hadn't already shared was my early sense that you needed a friend. I didn't want you to feel self-conscious about that, but wasn't my impulse to be furtive worse?

Twice I tucked the book back in its spot. The sense I would need it was too overwhelming—like I needed our emails and continued to save them, even after I had you 3-D and full-time. A day was coming when this book and photos would be all I had. When your voice sounded for me only in reading your emails. I could feel it like a truck bearing down, just out of sight. But how could I tell you I was hoarding memories for once you were gone? If I thought about it too long, my eyes welled with tears. So after my second moment of doubt, I accepted this secret.

We made more photo books, one for each year, filled with our travels and a few misadventures. I haven't made our 2017 book, sweetheart. I haven't had the heart. Our final road trip gave us great photos among Alcatraz cells and redwoods, saguaros and canyons. Your long arms made it easy to take great selfies of us, grinning and tucked close together. I keep telling myself I'll assemble that book for your birthday, our anniversary, the date of your death. But it would only have pages for two months, not a year, and I can't bring myself to design a last one.

Another book has taken its place, anyway—the leather-bound journal you bought me from a street vendor on our trip to New York. I wanted to use it immediately, not hide it on a shelf, but I didn't have the right words to put in it yet. Its beauty demanded my most heartfelt thoughts. It decorated my desk for a couple of years while I waited for the right inspiration.

Only on the day after you left did I see what that journal was for. Many of these words were first written there. But only after the *tick-ticking* of our love's clock had stopped.

How I Tried to Keep You (1)

My intense sense of time passing moved into my body in a vain attempt to control the hours. This compulsion began during my last visit to you, before your house purchase closed. As we settled to sleep after fiery lovemaking, I lay there holding my breath. For as long as I could. On the inhale I held it. On the exhale, too. *Stop. Don't inhale. Freeze. No ticking clock.* Our moments were rushing past with such merciless force.

Refusing to breathe, being there, being then was the best I could do to slow the river of time. If I could've stopped my heart's beating, too, I would have. Only that stillness anchored us, briefly, to stretch and preserve my great happiness. When I held my breath we slipped outside of time, where I could hold you forever—or until my effort failed. The word "spirit" comes from the Latin word for breath, and my lungs tried to hold our spirits together. Until my vision grew dim, my head light, and I had to relent.

The more I held my breath, the more attention I paid to yours, too. Snuggling against you every night confirmed something I'd noticed and wondered about. You never snored, but the pauses between your breaths while you slept occasionally seemed longer than normal. A few times I counted off up to ten seconds before you inhaled again. Previously I hadn't been certain, less familiar with your body and habits and rhythms, but a few weeks into living together, hearing that silence made it hard for me to relax. Had my sense that I wouldn't have you for long been prompted by a subconscious awareness and the fear that you might stop breathing completely?

Maybe, but that was a problem that could be fixed. My dad had used a CPAP machine for at least twenty years, so I knew about sleep apnea. Of course, he'd always snored like a bear, and you never did, but he claimed to feel much better once he started to use it.

Being a nag was a risk I could take. You even gave me a good opportunity when you mentioned that you needed to find a doctor to schedule a regular check-up, since your usual doctor was now too far away. I cheered in my head. Another way you defied the macho stereotype of men who refuse to visit a doctor!

Volunteering to find us each a doctor in our new town, I said, "Sweetheart, has anyone ever told you that you might have sleep apnea? It seems to me like you sometimes stop breathing for longer than you ought to at night."

"Really?" You seemed suitably impressed when I told you I could count to ten in the longest gaps. "Maybe that's why I feel tired lately, huh? It's not just you wearing me out every night?"

Despite the tease, you agreed to ask about it. I was relieved you didn't feel harangued.

Relief was also my primary emotion when you learned you did need a CPAP machine. Being wrong might have been nicer, but I was happy my suggestion would improve your sleep and your health. And it did, as your follow-up testing confirmed. You seemed to have little trouble getting used to the mask and hose we called your "schnozzle." It ran so quietly we both slept better.

"It's not very sexy," you sighed. Okay, maybe you went from a ten to a nine. But the fireworks were always over by the time you pulled it on, and it came off quickly enough on demand that it never got in the way of our snuggling.

But it didn't silence the ticking in the back of my heart, either. It should have reassured me like a bullet dodged. Instead it only proved you were mortal. I had to keep holding my breath while awake to smother the rush of our days speeding past. Stopping my breath became my go-to reaction every time joy and love overtook me and I yearned to stop right where we were. Almost daily. I refused to breathe while beside you in the truck, during concerts, at restaurants, as we went out for walks. And I particularly tried to stop time while cuddled against you. *Stop, time. Please stop. Please don't go so fast.* I prayed we'd die together, invoking a plane crash, a wreck on the freeway, a diving disaster.

Often this pleading squeezed tears from my eyes. You sometimes noticed, and I had to explain my tears. But I didn't want such perfect moments to be reduced to my fear of your death, so instead I told you how great my gratitude was, how overwhelming I found our love. That was utterly true, if not the full explanation. It was the light shorn away from the shadow behind it. You nodded and squeezed me and accepted that answer. Your eyes occasionally glistened in those moments, too.

I tried to tell myself this dread of the future wasn't rational. It was silly. I've never been a worrier, and it was stupid to start. *Stop feeling pangs over a future that hasn't happened!* I was probably imagining that pending loss. The ghost of my divorce might have even been roused, moaning to my heart that loss lay ahead now, too. But this love felt so different! In fact, after more than a decade, I'd finally forgiven past mistakes and people. My long-held resentment had dissipated when it occurred to me that without that wrenching break-up, I would never have known you or this depth of love. Even someone who'd hurt me deserved to feel it, or try. Enlightened, I tried to also cast off my foreboding. *Enjoy these sparkling moments, sure, but we'll have plenty more*—many years and likely decades together.

Cardinals chirped through my breath-holds. Your heart thumped under my cheek. Time didn't obey any more than my fear did.

Unable to stop time, we teamed up to mock it.

A Message from a Sponsor

C an't stop time? Think cosmetic surgery promotes the wrong values? Try new Acme Time-Reversal Elixir! No costly wrinkle cream or vitamin tonic, this all-natural solution returns even doomed lovers to youth. Apply nightly and watch daily activities become childlike. Works great around the house, in your truck, and in moments like these:

- Carving jack-o'-lanterns and making scary faces in their candlelight in the dark

- Dragging your kids' sled to the nearest slope and whooping so much you chase off the neighbor boys, embarrassed by old people taking over their sled run

- Camping out in a highly flammable tent with an electric heater taped to a dryer duct because you can't wait until the frost ends to sleep under the stars

- Retrieving model airplanes from the roof of the house and the landscaping of unamused neighbors

- Hunting for geocached treasure on beaches and in parks despite puzzled looks from other adults

- Collecting pretty rocks and dreaming of a rock tumbler for Christmas

- Watching hippos at zoos and riding attractions at Epcot Center even without a child in tow

- Pushing each other on the swing in the yard until motion-sickness nearly makes somebody puke

- Best of all, discovering the passion teenagers know. Defying the 36 percent of American adults* who feel awkward about public displays of affection to commit mild PDAs on every occasion.

Here's what one happy customer has to say about Acme:

Before I discovered Acme, I'd been burned by a man's reluctance to appear as a couple. My first weekend using Time-Reversal Elixir, I asked my new sweetheart, "Will you hold my hand in public?"

Implying the question was silly, he held my hand every day, on sidewalks and across restaurant tables. Much younger waiters, amused by our giddy love, fished for tips by commenting, "You guys are so cute!"

Even better, when we encountered a curb or small log, he often stopped and cleared his throat, waiting. When I stepped up to reduce the gap in our heights, he granted me a "curb kiss." Right there in public.

Thanks, Acme!

Not everyone can enjoy Acme Time-Reversal Elixir. The best candidates are people who follow their hearts. Side effects include honesty and vulnerability as well as laughter and joy. Check with your heart and see if you qualify to use this wondrous Elixir today!

*Based on a 2019 *Women's Health* survey. Not intended as medical advice. Ask your doctor if Acme Time-Reversal Elixir is right for you. Acme, Inc., makes no claim to prevent untimely death.

Kismet

More than once in my battle with time, destiny stepped in to give our love an advantage.

When you took the job in Ohio, you'd committed to staying for at least three years, and we expected to make it five. Eighteen months later, you changed your mind. Despite how clearly you loved the challenge of running the plant, you abruptly declared, "I'm going to retire. What would you think? We can go back to your house and travel around the West Coast."

No argument here! But what brought that on? You'd only just turned fifty-seven. Did you feel that *tick-ticking*, too?

"I just realized I can do it financially," you explained. "And I'm having too much fun with you to keep going to work."

Like everything else in our lives, once that choice had been made, events accelerated. We prepared to put the house on the market, thinning our possessions and painting. It had sat empty for two years before you bought it, and our agent, Sheila, said the market hadn't improved. Expecting a sale to take a year or longer, we began scheming a road trip to New England while we still lived on "your" side of the country. It would get us out of the house to facilitate showings and eliminate the need to drive across the whole country later to see distant places like Boston and Maine.

We didn't get beyond a wish-list of destinations. The house sold the day it listed. We had two offers. Cash.

I've had *way* too many experiences with house sales to doubt that they're ruled by fate. You get the house you were meant to and sell when it's destined, even if neither feels that way at first. Thank Real-Estate Kismet. Fate has saved me from what would've soon become awful decisions at least three times, two failed purchases and one failed sale. Plus our beloved home in the mountains came to me only after yet another purchase fell through. At the time, I was living like a wraith in a house my future ex wanted to keep but that I couldn't escape fast enough. I couldn't find a rental that wasn't a dump, and the sellers who'd taken my offer for their colorful cottage reneged when they discovered friends wanted to buy it instead. I went for a drive to cry in frustration and consider a midlife return to my parents. Turning around after twenty forested miles, I experienced my life's most intense déjà vu and then spotted a white three-by-five-inch index card on a ski cabin porch. (Really.) The déjà vu forced me out of my car to look closer. The card displayed a phone number and a scrawled, "For Sale by Owner." It was perfect for me, I could actually afford it, and the owner let me move in before our deal closed.

Despite my real estate fatalism, even I couldn't believe the speed of our Ohio sale. When our real estate agent called with two full-price offers, I thought she was joking. Auctions weren't yet a thing, the town was still crippled by the Great Recession, and she had prepared us to expect a long haul. Was this her way of saying the listing was live? She laughed and convinced me, and we'd spent enough time together previously for her to say something like, "You two are blessed!"

The buyer asked if we could be out in two weeks. I heard the Universe loud and clear: We were meant to get back to my West Coast cabin, pronto.

In the next couple of weeks, we packed everything that would fit into a single moving pod, giving away everything else. Most of it went to your son. After our last delivery to him, his Kentucky apartment resembled an episode of *Hoarders*. By then, six more spoons wouldn't have fit in our pod. Whistling our dogs into your canopied truck, we made up for our missed road trip with a long route back west, traversing Canada between Springfield and Seattle. We pulled into Washington in late June.

Although it hurts to count our love on my fingers, I appreciate the symmetry the Universe gave us: nineteen months in Ohio together, nineteen with you in Washington State. I'm intensely grateful you retired when you did. I got most of the time you would've given your work, which we shared traveling and playing and puttering around. You called it everything you'd imagined retirement could be—backpacking, woodworking, curling in front of the woodstove to read, camping on road trips, and beautifully remodeling our house. It pleased me to help make your retirement perfect. After a career of ten- and twelve-hour days, you'd earned it.

"I should've done it sooner," you said. While I wish you had, too, I'm more glad you leapt when you did. Some inner voice prompted, and you paid attention, heeding your heart as much as I heeded mine.

Lampyridae

The worst failing of Washington State is a climate that's hostile to *Lampyridae*. The name means "shining ones." Non-Latin speakers call them fireflies.

Ohio has twelve species. The shining ones in our Springfield yard were probably the most common, known as big dipper fireflies. The pond in the meadow behind us spawned dozens, which blinked up from the grass on dry summertime evenings and slowly moved into the trees. We often sat on the porch in the evening to greet them until the mosquitos got bad. After rising at night for the bathroom, I frequently leaned on the windowsill to gaze out before returning to bed. In the deeper blackness of those magical hours, with frogs burbling beyond the window screen, the fireflies bobbed as thick as snowflakes and burned as brightly as sparks.

Fireflies blink to find firefly love. Some species sync up to glow together. Watching them from beside you or while you waited in bed made me feel inexpressibly lucky. Bioluminescence wasn't needed for me to glow, too.

After we moved away from firefly country, twinkle lights on our porch had to do. White LEDs paled alongside the real thing but still made me smile at memories.

We say dog years amount to seven years for a person. No one compares human time to a firefly's life. Their days are too numbered.

No one but me. Adult fireflies typically live less than four weeks.

As it turned out, a shining firefly's week was the equivalent of each bright year with you.

East Coasters seem to take fireflies for granted. Maybe my delight in such ephemeral magic was my soul's way to honor the hard truth I knew. You can't keep fireflies. If you jar them, they die. Pay attention, because you can only enjoy them while lit. After that, their shining has to live in your heart.

Like I'm Gonna Lose You

O ur first summer together in Washington, I heard a new song.

Artist: Meghan Trainor
Album: *Title*
Label: Epic
Track: six
Single release date: June 23, 2015

Halfway across our living room, I stopped in my tracks at the first few lines of *Like I'm Gonna Lose You*. I leaned there near the stereo speaker to follow the lyrics more closely. Trainor's words pricked tears that first time, and most every time after.

I'm gonna love you like I'm gonna lose you. That pledge had been locked in my heart without words. Now, just as we'd settled into a new routine, it spilled into our house over radio waves, a fresh reminder to be grateful. The album was the first item on my Christmas list that December. The lyrics resonated too deeply—although not for some critics, one of whom called it "smarm." Color me smarmy, but for me they were true, and they stung less when I could lean against you or squeeze your big hand. I often sang the words to myself under my breath: *I'm gonna hold you like we're saying good-bye.* Gratitude flooded me each time we hugged, both for you and the cue not to grow complacent.

The Universe bestowed a second stroke of mercy the following fall. That's how it felt at the time, anyway. A few days after our second Cozumel dive trip, you got the call you'd expected for years. Lynetta's poor body was finally failing. You'd flown back to see her and your son several times since we'd moved, but this time you didn't schedule a return flight.

The nursing staff told you it was a matter of days. She hung on though, her organs still fighting, while you remained on death watch for weeks, over Thanksgiving. Our daily FaceTime connections displayed your exhaustion, which made my heart ache. I longed to be stashed in your B&B room, hidden from your kids except to hold you each night. Your son had spent several weekends with us, and even your daughter had been civil, given no choice. Eventually we'd shared meals with her in Maui. Still, we all knew my presence at her mother's death wouldn't help—even if that death was mostly a technicality by then.

More than once after dealing with alarms over Lynetta's care, from billing mistakes to stubborn bedsores, you'd murmured into my shoulder, "Why? Why is she still here, holding on?" Then your guilt would speak, too. "That's terrible, isn't it? But like I told my son, his mom was gone long ago. Years." Such feelings weren't terrible, merely humane. On the visits I'd made to her care home with you, her body had looked like a hand-colored photo of a concentration camp victim. Nothing and nobody in her surroundings provoked even a flicker of her half-lidded eyes. She was like a rag doll to roll over or touch. And another two years passed before her body finally gave in.

It wasn't that her care wasn't capable. The staff were, if anything, too attentive, too willing to stuff her body with calories, fluids, and drugs she'd long since lost the ability to take in herself—sometimes in direct violation of orders, finding ways to bypass her clenched teeth and then acting wounded when you didn't approve. Dementias don't always play out so badly, but that home for end-stage Alzheimer's patients was little more than a well-decorated warehouse for corpses who didn't know enough not to breathe.

When Lynetta's empty body finally stopped fighting, you arranged for a service and wanted old family photos to display. You asked me to pull images from your old laptop to send you. Happy to help, I took my time sorting through photos, many of which I'd seen before.

You were a beautiful couple, sweetheart. Tall, blonde, and pretty, she was such a better match for your good looks than I was. The first time you'd shared some of those images with me, I'd drawn information about you from them. This time, looking through made me feel schizophrenic. I smiled at your youth and the playfulness I adored, but it hurt to have missed so many years of your life. I'd never stood proudly alongside as you sported a tux, young and sassy and incredibly handsome, or cuddled a baby with you, or laughed over kids of our own. Those moments sorting photos for you were easily the most jealous I've lived.

Oh—as I'm writing this, I look up. My stomach's been churning at these memories while I pretend to eat lunch at The Kettle. We shared so many brunch omelets at this little farm restaurant, but I didn't realize it played background music. The notes of Meghan Trainor's "Like I'm Gonna Lose You" just broke through the voices and my concentration. Thank you, sweetie. I hope it means you forgive me for the phone call we had after you received my FedEx package containing a flash drive of photos.

When your name and face appeared on my phone that afternoon, unexpected, I was driving and had just reached the McDonald's where we got drinks almost daily. Overjoyed, I parked and answered.

"Thank you for the photos, hon," you said. "You did a great job. Picked out some good ones. The kids are happy to see them."

"There were so many nice ones, it was hard to decide what to send." Tears suddenly rose, and you heard my voice tighten.

"Is something wrong?" you asked.

"No," I said, but my tears turned it into that voice we all recognize as a lie. And we were always so honest. I had to explain. My left hand tightened hard on the steering wheel, too late to turn back or keep my turmoil hidden. "I just—I admit it made me feel jealous. I'm jealous of all the years she had with you."

You sighed. "I'm sorry. I shouldn't have asked that of you."

"No, I was happy to do it," I protested. That, too, was true. "I . . . I just miss you." You'd been gone so much longer than we had expected.

"I'll be home soon," you replied, and we ended the call. But I cried in the car before driving on, feeling like I'd damaged our love and your trust. It was starting to feel like you weren't coming back, that your old life had reclaimed you and I'd already lost you.

Later that week as I approached home, I had a weird impulse to stop for a jalapeño burger for dinner. Hamburgers hadn't been part of my diet for a decade—not since the grim years immediately after my divorce. I didn't obey that bizarre impulse, but in pondering it, I decided it was a mild PTSD flashback. You'd been gone so long, through such roiling emotions, that my sense of abandonment after my divorce had returned, along with that impulse for self-medication.

Now I wonder if it wasn't a flash-forward instead, a premonition of the grief of soon living without you.

At last the memorial service for Lynetta was done. When you came home a few days later, I apologized for failing you. You protested again that it wasn't my job. Maybe not, but we were partners, sweetheart. That's the meaning of the Macintosh ring you bought me in Scotland, which is on my ring finger intentionally. Like the designs of that artist team, you and I were mirror reflections, and I should've supported you better.

You still looked rough when I met you at the airport, but your face and heart brightened immediately. My Tony 2.0 had returned. With the loss of Lynetta more finally behind you, you began planning our future more avidly than before. Trips to Australia and Greece appeared on our calendar, as well as a winter road trip to Southwestern sun.

Marriage crossed my mind, but I didn't voice it. Such a step was too soon for your grieving kids. Instead I just kept holding my breath. And your hand.

The Math of a Compassionate Universe

 7 dive trips
+ 1 pizza debt (paid)
+ 9 countries, 26 states, 4 provinces
+ 19,374.7 North American road trip miles
+ 12 outdoor sports, some more comedic than athletic
+ $17,450 (estimated, before tax) in Home Depot charges
+ 1,200 nights minimum snuggling into your arms to sleep

---

 42 months or one infinite moment of love

Fond Plans to Grow Old

You were so proud of the spreadsheets you'd created to track your retirement account, which you'd nursed to an impressive size. Once you no longer had to subtract the cost of Lynetta's care, the math simplified. You clearly loved plotting scenarios for it, changing which month you started drawing from it and how much we might spend traveling. When you worked on those charts, I usually made myself scarce. After all, I had a minor reputation to live down.

Your friends were protective. In our first months together, I had met several, and we later spent holidays with the dearest, Dennis and Mamie, in Florida. Early in our relationship, more than one of these friends warned I might be a "gold digger." The sundress I wore for my first introduction prompted one couple to say, "Isn't she a little young for you?" When you shared that, we laughed about the four years between us somehow disqualifying me. Maybe they found me silly! But honestly, their concern was warranted and only reflected their caring. You were successful, your wounded heart vulnerable, and our relationship progressed at warp speed. I would've questioned my motives, too.

Still, I appreciated a comment your brother had made. He caught me at my first visit to your siblings near Cleveland, which I had been nervous about. You had admitted you weren't sure how they'd react, since Lynetta had been part of the family for so many years.

We drove up from Springfield to spend a weekend with them our first winter together in Ohio. They were pleasant enough over dinner. Your older brother displayed a dry sense of humor and played at being the family's patriarch, though tensions occasionally flickered between you. Probably left over from childhood wounds. Your smart older sister, Lynn, served as the heart of the family. The curious similarity between her name and Lynetta's soon faded into the pleasure of being with her. Your younger sister echoed something of your playfulness. Even without your younger brother there, I enjoyed the glimpse into the family dynamics that had formed you and the complementary tones of their respective spouses. Your middle-child diplomacy made me smile.

Then, as we were leaving, you stepped into the driveway while I was still slipping on my shoes near the door. Your oldest brother approached me.

"I wasn't going to say anything," he said softly.

I tensed, expecting to be chastised or warned off.

"It's been a long time since I've seen a smile on my brother's face," he continued. "Thank you."

That sounded sweeter than "gold digger" did.

Though we joked about what a lousy gold digger I was when we found nothing to buy after browsing gift shops, I cherished the trust you gave me, opening your finances as wide as your heart. Our last winter, you sat at the dining room table, playing with the retirement account charts on your laptop, and said with a laugh, "Forget my kids. No inheritance. You and I are spending every dime, hon. Come and look."

As I stepped toward you from the kitchen, you added, "So how old should I enter for life expectancy to set the date it runs out?"

Ugh. A dilemma. That bargain again. I raced through potential answers, grabbing my tea from the counter to cover the delay.

Before I met you, I'd dreaded old age, fearing decrepitude far

more than death. The bonus years I'd been granted after age thirty
had started to feel more lonely than lucky.

You erased that fear. I had you to grow old with! After the rejection explicit in my divorce, I'd sworn that I'd never marry again. You
changed my mind. I wanted to be your wife, sweet. For the symbolism, the statement to each other.

First we had to wait until Lynetta was gone. That was necessary
not only for the cost of her care but also your history and the obligation you felt. After she died, it seemed best to wait a bit more. Your
daughter tolerated me, but not gladly, and that final loss was still raw.
For another year, maybe, "soulmate" had to do. Thank you for saying
that word first.

But the truth of our relationship slipped now and then. In offhand
comments, you referred to yourself as "your hubby." Halfway through
a sentence I still hear myself say "my first husband." Technically, I've
only had one. But you are the one who counted. Neither of us corrected the waiters and clerks who assumed I was your wife because
we so often held hands.

So of course we'd grow into an old married couple. We'd take
care of each other, me pushing your wheelchair when your bad knees
finally went, you hooking (and unhooking!) my bra strap when my
shoulders got too stiff to reach around that far. The decades of your
life that I'd missed made me wistful, but they'd burnished you into
the man I loved. The path forward was sweet.

Could I hope for our seventies? If I suggested you plug seventy-five
into your spreadsheet, would I have to explain why I wasn't giving
you the benefit of the average male lifespan? But no, I wanted at least
thirty years. My bargain could apply after that, couldn't it?

"Ninety," I said, touching your shoulder in a benediction.

"Come on," you replied, dubious.

"You told me your aunt is nearly a hundred! You've got good genes, better than mine, and we're healthier than practically anyone I know. Including my friends who are a decade younger."

"Hmm." You pulled your lips to the side in your patented expression of wry amusement. "How about eighty-five?"

You assigned more money for travel than I thought we'd spend, so I didn't mind you shorting yourself that five years. After the click of an Excel button or two, you turned the laptop screen toward me. We admired the gentle downward slope of your hoard. It helped that we'd been running on savings and my income so you could leave it untouched until you reached fifty-nine and a half. No point in paying for early withdrawals. So you needn't take your first for several more months.

You never did. After working so hard all your life, paying all those taxes, earning all those 401(k) contributions, funding so many years of care for Lynetta, you enjoyed retirement for less than two years and spent not a dime of that fund.

I hate that despite my heightened awareness, I questioned your eagerness to travel so often. I didn't want to credit your inner clock about that. As we sat by an evening fire, you constantly asked, "When are we going diving again?" Or "How about another long road trip next month?" We talked about spending three months in Dominica. You checked airfares and picked out places to stay. We mused about various overseas cities where you could meet that career goal of international life but—even better—without having to work. I suggested Edinburgh. You said, "What about Japan?"

Although enticed and willing to leave the planet with you—fire up the rocket and hand me my spacesuit—I wanted to wait a year, maybe two, until both of our old dogs were gone. Months at a time in boarding seemed unfair to them. Leaving them at all made me feel guilty. Unlike your dog Bape, Jazz hated to travel, and he'd already endured two cross-country trips. It was wrong to repay him by abandoning him. Putting the dogs ahead of your wishes wasn't right either, but the shorter trips we were taking every few months seemed like a good compromise. We were about to escape the March rain with four weeks in Australia. Besides, you were making our home so gorgeous, from the knotty-pine dormers to the airy new staircase. We had to stay home to enjoy it.

Plus the warning in my heart had grown fainter, muted by reason and sheer time together. Our new loft and bedroom, where you'd added a bathroom, still needed mirrors and towel hooks and heat when you agitated to move our bed there and start using the space. Our Australia trip was less than two weeks away, but you wanted to enjoy that new plumbing the moment it worked.

It hurts to remember the thought that crossed my mind as we set up the bedframe in the paint fumes: *What's the rush?* Stupid, really. I'm glad I never said it. Deep down, I knew.

How I Tried to Keep You (2)

You were gasping and choking. It woke me. We'd both gotten out of bed to use the bathroom by then, me around two o'clock and you sometime after. I'd been vaguely aware of you sliding back into bed alongside me. Then about 4:40 a.m., a loud groaning broke through my sleep. You had nightmares sometimes, often flinging an arm or a leg as you battled demons. You lay on your stomach. I touched your back to nudge you out of the dream.

You didn't start quickly awake as usual, but went on making those strangled shouts and then lifting yourself off your chest in the struggle to breathe. I think now your heart must've stopped, and your brain was doing everything it knew to find oxygen. Getting louder and rougher, I kept trying to rouse you, not computing for a moment why you weren't waking up. Shaking you hard, calling your name, then yelling, "Wake up! Tony, *wake up!*"

Your CPAP seemed to be working, with its usual soft whoosh. Its alarm hadn't gone off. I yanked the mask off your head anyway and shook you again. "Tony! You're scaring me—okay, I'm calling 911." Maybe the threat of an embarrassing intervention would snap you out of it.

I grabbed the cordless phone by the bed. I'd never before used it. Before or after I dialed, or maybe while the connection went through, I don't know, I jumped up, hit the light, and jumped back to you. I rolled you onto your back, not understanding why your eyes were clenched shut. And they *were* clenched, not just closed. I pried up your right eyelid.

Your right eye was horribly empty. I knew from its blankness that you were unconscious, if not, in retrospect, already gone. When the 911 operator answered, I asked for an ambulance. You had stopped breathing. A calm woman's voice asked if you had a pulse.

Dutifully I pressed my fingertips against your left jugular, but honestly, I couldn't feel my fingers. I had no idea if you had no pulse or I was simply too stressed to feel it.

"I don't think so."

We were going to do CPR, she told me. I replied that I'd had some training. Punching the speakerphone function, I set the phone on the nightstand, out of the way.

She instructed me to get you on a hard surface. Rolling you onto your back had been easy—maybe because you were pushing yourself up anyway. Getting you off the bed was another matter. Pulling your arms didn't work, not with the drag of bedding against your 220 pounds. I yanked and tugged at your body, trying to find leverage. Jesus, I'd taken ten years of jujitsu. I'd thrown men your size! Why couldn't I drag your limp form three feet?

Finally I pulled on your legs to dump you off the bed, none too gently. By then I worried only about not cracking your head on the floor. You'd gone quiet.

I quickly swept your half-open mouth with a finger, remembering that lesson to clear it, though it's not like it applied. You hadn't choked on a meal. I pinched your Italian nose, covered your mouth, and blew into you before starting compressions.

Getting compression on you was *so* much harder than training had prepared me for. The 911 operator wanted them an inch deep, and the only way I could budge your big chest at all was to straddle you and use my whole body, rising above you with all of my weight balanced over my hands. Only the tops of my feet stayed on the ground. I knew, as a result, I was going too slow, less than a compression per second. But an insufficient compression would be worthless. That seemed worse.

I twisted to give you a breath every three or four compressions. Air forced back out by the compressions made noises. At first I hoped they were you trying to breathe.

"Come on, Tony. Please?"

The operator had mentioned help on the way, but I knew it would be at least fifteen minutes. Our home in Greenwater is a long way from civilization. As I kept smashing your chest, still warm and ruddy, the operator said I should be hearing sirens. That I should stop long enough to go unlock the door. Flying downstairs, I flipped the latch and raced back up.

No sirens. Still no sirens. Midway through compressions, I glanced at the clock. It'd been twenty minutes. And then twenty five. I asked for an ETA.

"They're coming," she said.

I never did hear sirens, only the crunch of tires on our deep snow. Feet pounded the wood porch. A fist battered the door.

"Upstairs!" My scream came out hoarse. Not hearing an entry, I jumped up again, yanked my robe from its hook, and dragged it around me as I skipped stairs back down. The team, burdened with gear, was only testing the door as I reached it. Mentally I cursed them for not trying it sooner, for making me leave you to usher them in.

Was it silly of me to not burst down there nude?

Spinning, I ran back up upstairs. Three or four of our volunteer firefighters followed. They immediately, so easily, moved you into the loft, where they had more room to work than alongside our bed.

"Do you have a defibrillator?" I asked. I'd started writing for a famous defib manufacturer, so I knew too much about the process. Painfully too much.

The odds, for instance: fewer than ten percent. And most of

those are in a hospital setting. The movies and TV are unrealistic. Especially after so long, with a poor oxygen supply. . . .

No. Don't think any more about that.

I hovered and watched, frustrated and helpless. Their pro compressions didn't seem deep enough; there was no way your breastbone was moving an inch. They applied the defib. So hopeful, that first shock!

And the second one, too.

The oxygen bottle they held over your face didn't seem to make your chest rise. Litter from epinephrine injections lay all around. I touched your left foot. It was starting to cool.

The phone beeped from the nightstand. Nine-one-one had hung up.

"At least the analysis is still finding rhythm to shock," one of the EMTs told me after about the third or fourth shock. By then I had lost all but the last grains of hope. Out of the way on the floor, I curled up on myself, watching. Suspended in time. Knowing it was over, that "together" was done. I sensed your arms around my shoulders from behind, comforting me. Or apologizing. I wanted to feel you; I hope I wasn't making that up.

A second response team had arrived after the first, crowding too many people in our little loft. CPR teams traded off. More epi, more oxygen, more compressions. More shocks. Six total—I've never heard of them doing that many.

Finding my cell phone, I texted my mom. And then called. It rolled over to voice mail. Of course. It wasn't yet 6:00 a.m. on a Sunday.

"I'm sorry to wake you so early a second day in a row," I said. She'd complained about someone's early call the previous morning. "But Tony stopped breathing. EMTs are here, but it doesn't look good. Can you come?"

She scolded me later for apologizing. I was simply still operating in a normal world. My brain couldn't grasp the new one I'd entered.

My mother was unprepared for this reality, too. She called back before hearing my message, awakened by my missed call.

"Mom, Tony's gone," I told her.

"To Ohio?" Her assumption reflected not only my word choice but her fears. She later explained, "You were so clearly smitten I was terribly worried that for Tony it was a 'shipboard romance' and he'd break your heart."

Yours had failed instead, but the result was the same: You'd left me. I had to explain you were dead.

Knowing my parents were on the way made it real. No mirage. No escape. Before the EMTs finished, I said, "You could probably stop." They'd already worked on you nearly an hour, from just past five until after six. Not counting the thirty minutes I'd breathed into you. They had a protocol to follow, they told me. Whoever they were consulting on their radios had to call it.

When they finally stopped, someone spread the wool throw we'd brought from Ohio over your nude body. It looked so defenseless, so tender. So empty. You were long gone. Your cool foot was graying by then. I stroked it anyhow. That last brush of your skin.

The responders tried to comfort me. A hand on my back, an arm around my shoulder. One of them said that I'd done all I could. As if I didn't know, hadn't the bruises to prove it, the backs of both hands marked by my effort. It was the next day before I noticed the bloody scrapes on the tops of my feet. They'd rubbed against the plank floor as I'd pressed on your chest, but adrenaline and stress had kept the raw places painless until my socks stuck to the wounds.

I was numb, crushed and numb at the same time, which doesn't make sense until you've been there. I think I'd known even while I performed CPR that it was over. You were gone. I was running on autopilot, that's all. Autopilot and futile hope.

There's one thing, though, sweetheart, that I haven't told anyone else. Something that both puzzles me and sears me with shame.

While pressing on your chest, watching your face for the least sign of life, an alien thought had appeared in my head.

If this doesn't work, I guess you can start running again.

Before leaving Springfield, we'd raced in a fun run together. To our shock, we both won medals for our age groups. (One advantage of a small town: less competition.) Recently, though, we'd agreed to limit ourselves to hiking and biking because the pain in your knees had gotten too bad. You hated being the reason we stopped. You kept apologizing. I tried to tell you hiking was enough. That anything outdoors with you was enough. You seemed to think running mattered more to me than it did.

That's why I'm unsure that internal voice was mine, and not yours. Shocked by the random and selfish idea, I growled mentally, *Shut up!* And kept compressing your chest. Screw running. I would've cut my legs off with your circular saw if I could've chosen between them and you.

The thought that I could start running again returned a few minutes later, insistent.

"Is that your idea, Tony? Shut the fuck up!" That time I said it aloud.

My brain went mercifully silent again, focused on trying to make you be alive. I don't know if that voice was some perverse part of me, trying to see a bright side to my life's biggest disaster even as it unfolded. God, sweetheart, I hope not. I'd rather I told *you* to fuck off. For that particular suggestion, you would deserve it.

By the time the responders stopped trying, too, only a rushing void filled my head. It was hard to look at you, still with me but not, especially once they'd picked you up in a sheet for the awkward transit downstairs.

Paperwork then. Questions. Your age, what had happened, what medications you took. The medicine question I answered three or four times. I had to get out the bottles to show them. I think they wanted the list to be longer. But they weren't interested in your CPAP machine or its data. Most of the responders then left, but two waited with me for the medical examiner. Which took fucking forever, more than another hour with your poor body laid out on our living room floor.

One of the two who stayed was a local guy, Mike. In addition to once owning Greenwater's quaint general store, he'd lived on our cul-de-sac some years before. He'd once helped me put out a small chimney fire. He and his colleague sank into chairs, turning them toward where I hunched near the floor.

His familiar face grounded that dizzying wait. (I also made tea for us all while we waited and lit a fire in the woodstove to warm our chilly dawn house. I don't know how I did such normal things.) He'd lost a wife to cancer, so I thought he might have wisdom to share.

Curled over the hollow warmth of my mug, I broke the silence. "Any advice, Mike?"

"Stay busy," he said. The silence resumed.

I studied the bruises CPR left on my hands. His advice seemed moronic. Chores were going to replace you? You had changed who I was, what I believed about life. You were the fire in my heart. A fire quenched. I should just vacuum more often?

That's enough of this memory. It hurts too much to linger. The medical examiner arrived with more paperwork, more syllables of sympathy from kindly strangers. If you don't know about those details, too, you don't care. Either you've reached a state of complete understanding—or, since my convictions are hardly airtight, you are void, way beyond hearing my words.

If I didn't have so much painful proof of your absence, I wouldn't quite believe that morning was real. It seems more like a grim novel scene I might write, dreaming it up to torture myself.

It's easy to feel I could've done something different. If I had realized faster that you weren't dreaming, had less trouble getting you onto the floor, started CPR sooner, pumped faster, *something*, it might have made a difference. But I don't think it would. I believe you were already out of your body when you stopped making noises. If not before then.

I'm glad you never woke up. I'm sure you were asleep when the blood stopped reaching your brain. And then you were unconscious. And then watching me, maybe, from somewhere over my head, while I worked so hard to keep you alive. You slid out so easy, without panic or pain. Those were reserved for me.

But I did feel you there, empathizing with me, for the half hour in which I thought I might convince you to breathe. Even if I *had* shouted an obscenity at you.

And I remembered so clearly the previous night, when we'd held each other close. As usual, I'd been holding my breath.

"I love you, Joni," you'd murmured. Your voice, raw and intimate, sounded my name. We acted on our feelings every day, but we didn't say the words so often. That conserved their meaning.

The stillness in my lungs when you said it for the last time made it easier to hear both your words and our hearts. Thank you so, Tony, for saying good-bye.

PART 4

AFTER

Laundry

Around noon, as I passed through our hallway, my fingertips flew to my lips. They couldn't hold the sensation there—the knowledge I'd had Tony's last kiss.

The last one.

Even that hurt less than the blow an hour later. Mom, trying to be helpful, pulled Tony's socks from the dryer and dropped them into an empty cardboard box. *Thud.*

It could've been the sound of my collapsing heart.

Instructions for
Bereaved Robots

1. Approve organ donation. Answer weird questions about Tony's medical history and wonder what the answers have to do with his corneas anyway.

2. Call Tony's sisters and oldest friends. Sit on the stool near the floor so hearing it in my own voice, over and over, doesn't drop me. Cringe at their cheery, unsuspecting greetings. Close my eyes against the gasps and floundering after I speak.

3. Reply on his phone to panicked texts from his niece, who can't believe what she's heard.

4. Find his twenty-five-year-old will. Wish he'd updated it to make me his executor instead of muttering, "I need to get that done" for six months.

5. Fulfill his desire for organ donation and cremation, despite his family's agitation about them. Be glad the medical examiner did not make me prove it, but don't regret telling her I was his wife.

6. Request refunds for our trip to Australia and submit the thirty pages of paperwork they demand. (Note for law enforcement officials: If I ever take an assault rifle into a building, it'll be the

one in California that holds our travel insurance office.) Never buy travel insurance again. It's a scam.

7. Get the death certificate and the medical examiner's phone call with the cause: an enlarged heart. Try to make people believe he'd had no symptoms, no signs.

8. Call our doctor in case the news could help him save someone else. And maybe to make him feel guilty. "I'm so sorry," he will say, shuffling papers on the other end of the phone. "I've looked back over his file. I still see nothing that would have suggested he had a problem."

9. Decide Tony's big heart was broken by Lynetta's illness, and that he and I were just graced with a few years' delay.

10. Donate money to our volunteer firefighters for trying so hard to extend that grace.

11. Remind myself how fate and intuition served us, and that what counts most continues unseen between us. Try to feel as though that is enough.

Racking them up and knocking them off was the only way to survive.

Ghost

No.
It's not the one who dies who's a ghost.
It's the one who is left—
Or not one
Half only,
Alive and alone;
Adrift through the days,
Crying softly at night.

But the half left behind
Is also the haunted,
Waking up trembling
A part in the bed,
Heart pounding like yours once did
Under my cheek.

And the ghost is our house, too.
Hollow and leaning
Abandoned
Careening.
I'd welcome a ghost.
Will you please come and haunt me?
I'm not scared of the dead

Or of death, but of breath.

What frightens me most is the future.

Together, conjoined

Apart, only shards

Biding the time till reunion again.

Sometimes I feel you comforting me.

Others, I only survive the next moment

For you: both our hearts beating now in my chest.

I wasn't surprised to get the report.

Of course your heart was enlarged:

It had all of mine in it.

~ Your dove

(you already know that I love you)

Haunting

"I don't like ghosts." Tony said this more than once in a little-kid voice, with a pout and a shiver. His reaction to snakes was nearly the same. Any mention of ghosts, snakes, or eels drew the same grimace—part amusement, part "eek!"—but he still ogled eels I pointed out underwater and dealt calmly with snakes we encountered on trails. So when he said things like, "Don't tell me any stories with ghosts!" I never could tell how much he was kidding.

Maybe not much. He playfully put his hands over his ears when I started to describe the spooks at my grandmother's house. Raised Catholic, he may have absorbed the faith's conflation of snakes and demons, grouping ghosts with the latter. The church had lost him, however, when he looked for comfort during Lynetta's illness. The priest he'd made an appointment to speak with made him feel guilty for needing support in the face of "God's will."

"All he wanted to talk about was himself and Notre Dame football," Tony recalled.

When he recounted that experience for me, it confirmed my bias against organized religion, but it also revealed that until recently he'd retained more faith than a lot of people raised Catholic. I don't know his beliefs about an afterlife, though, or how much they conformed to Catholic dogma. He evaded my tentative efforts to find out, although I tried more than once. It may well be the one topic we never discussed, and it's one of my only regrets that I don't know what he expected when he went to discover the truth.

Ghosts must be less scary from that side, however, because at first I routinely felt Tony's presence. At least one of these visitations left evidence.

Special Evidence

A handful of hours had passed since Tony had gone. The moment the medical examiner pulled away, Mom suggested we drive to town to feed my dad breakfast. When we returned, I zombie-walked across the living room to stir up the fire in the woodstove. As I crossed back toward my tea kettle, I stopped and stared. An extra-large Hershey's Special Dark chocolate bar sat against the TV.

Unnerved, I scanned the rest of the room. Had someone come inside while we were gone? An identical Special bar also lay at Tony's end of the couch, where he'd read every evening.

Goosebumps. These were from him. *Special* was a code word between us. He'd constantly referred to gifts I'd given him, a raincoat and headphones and a radio-controlled plane, as things "someone special gave me." This habit had emerged from whispered sweet nothings that bordered on a gentle tug-of-war.

"You are so special, Tony."

"No, I'm just a guy who works in a factory. You're the one who's special. You make me feel lucky."

We'd eventually agreed we were special together, and dark chocolate was our official state fruit.

My head buzzing, I moved toward the nearest candy bar at the TV. The set had been Tony's before he met me. Since he and I almost never watched it, I didn't even know which remote turned it on. Was that mysterious chocolate bar real? It might vanish, like he had. Scared to touch it, I forced myself to reach out.

It was real. Heavy. The plastic wrapper was cool. I wanted to press its solid length to my heart, letting it melt directly into my chest, but not with my parents there—oh! There was another! A third bar gleamed brown and red near the far end of the room, propped against Tony's computer. Three quarter-pound Special Darks had appeared in our house, in the three places I most associated with him, other than upstairs on his side of the bed. Where we'd spent too much painful time that morning.

He'd sent them as a last proof of his love, an acknowledgement that we had something special. And sweet.

Did he have human help? He had rarely locked any of our homes for short jaunts. Particularly here in the woods, a bear was more likely to come in than a burglar, and Tony had teased me enough for fumbling for the key that after three years with him, I'd broken the habit. When I left with my parents, I hadn't locked up. Someone— one of the emergency responders, perhaps?—could have barged in with chocolate in hand.

But literally no one else knew Tony was gone yet. Most of our cul-de-sac's other houses are weekend ski rentals, and our friendliest neighbors were then snowbirding three states away. Plus it was still before nine o'clock on a Sunday morning. Maybe some early riser I didn't know heard from the paramedics what had happened, bought three giant candy bars without even knowing how I felt about chocolate, let themselves into our house uninvited, and planted the bars in three different, but meaningful, locations that were *not* the table or the kitchen counter, both of which are nearer the door and more logical places for food, without leaving a note or ever calling to explain.

Yeah, right. Who would do that? Invade the home of a woman who'd just suffered a traumatic loss? That wouldn't be compassionate. That's known as creepy. I'd find it pretty damn offensive, too—as if candy from an anonymous stranger could somehow soothe the loss? "Hi, you don't know me, but sorry the love of your life died. Have some chocolate." Just *no*. That is not remotely the equivalent of leaving a casserole on the porch.

I asked the one person I thought might've done that, our neighbor the cop, who'd seen all the aid car traffic that morning and who, for vocational reasons, might have a different attitude about entering without a warrant. He didn't know anything about any chocolate. Since he'd waited until he saw Mom's car pull back into the driveway before walking over, knocking, and handing me a lasagna and a pie from his freezer, his denial rang true. He'd been watching for us to return, so he'd probably have seen anyone else come to the house.

The emergency response team did drop off flowers—two days later, leaving them on the porch with a note. Like civilized people.

So perhaps Tony prompted some random stranger with an irresistible impulse to buy and deliver three extra-large chocolate bars. In that case, the Specials were still from Tony.

Grateful, I framed them. Seeing them comforted me, and they remind me of things we don't understand and that can feel pretty dark but nevertheless are both real and special.

That reminder gave me a lifeline to grasp. Intuition, that premonition of loss, had spurred me to love him as loud as I could and appreciate every day of our limited time. The question that remained for me once he was gone was whether similar attention to the unseen—to spirit—could help me survive the grief about to crush me.

Infinite Vistas

Our bed presented excruciating decisions—as it had all that miserable day Tony left. Keeping busy with laundry, Mom had offered to change the bedsheets for me.

"No!" I flinched, closer to panic than I'd been that day. She may have assumed I'd be creeped out, since he'd more or less died in our bed. On the contrary, I needed to keep his smell and touch on our bedding so I could sidle into the very space where he'd existed and wrap the comfort of his body around me.

She blinked at my vehemence but didn't argue.

She also bit her tongue, judging by her expression, when I pulled Tony's 2XL Ohio State sweatshirt from the back of his chair, where it hung. My family is not very demonstrative, though, and I needed holding. Oversized or not, like him, it held me snug.

That afternoon I went upstairs several times. First to clean up medical waste the EMT team had missed. While there I straightened the bed, pulling the blankets and duvet up smoothly. That was mostly to discourage Mom from defying my wishes and changing the sheets anyway, but it also felt like swaddling our intimacy there to save and protect it for later. Our bed, the floor alongside, the rug in the loft where he'd lain as the EMTs shocked him—none were as hard to look at as I might have expected. The new construction glowed too much with our love, with our hours and hours of working on it together, to be sullied by a mere moment in time.

The view and decisions got harder that night. I knew lying awake in our bed, with its miles of emptiness of him, would destroy me. But my mother had offered to stay a few nights and I needed to let her sleep even if I couldn't. In the hope that exhaustion might knock me out, I waited past midnight to go upstairs to lie down.

Tony and I had slept nude together, but nakedness now felt too vulnerable. Previously when we'd been apart, one of his gigantic T-shirts served as my sleepwear. I'd asked for one at the end of our very first weekend together so I could enjoy a second-hand sense of his skin even when we weren't together. Those makeshift pajamas now spoke too loudly of absence. I kept on my clothes and Tony's red sweatshirt, pulling it close as I flipped off the light.

The darkness helped hide the room's emptiness, but my feet didn't move. Another pointed decision: my side of our bed or his? Mine was forbidding, tainted by scrambling, alarm, the phone, 911. And farther away. I wanted to keep it that way.

But changing my spot loomed, a capitulation. It would acknowledge that my life had changed forever, shrunk in ways I wasn't yet able to grasp. I hadn't expected bedtime to force such an admission. Or maybe I'd been fleeing that admission all day and here, in the dark, it caught up.

Leaving wasn't an option, either. This room, those blankets, these intimate shadows were where Tony felt closest. So which would it be?

If I took my side, his empty place would yawn wider.

I gave up our teamwork, our play, and our future. Lifting the blankets, I crawled in on his side, where he hadn't awakened that morning—and so, in a sense, was still there. Clutching a second sweatshirt of his to my chest, I buried my face in his pillow, in the scent of his neck. The hollow carved by his body held me.

My eyelids, although drooping, wouldn't stay shut. I kept finding myself on my back, arms flung out crucifix style, staring blankly at the glowing stars we'd stuck on our ceiling. Dim vinyl proxies for the stars we'd shared in Hawaii, they reminded me of the bargain I'd made, as indifferent to my hollowing out as to a sacrifice on a stone altar.

Splayed there in abject surrender, that night and so many others to follow, I found moments of calm in my helplessness. There was nothing I could do. Not even think. *Out of Service. Please Pardon Our Disruption.* In this vacuum, tranquility sometimes felt just out of reach. Now and then, thin sleep descended. I'd wake up an hour later, shaken conscious by my own trembling. Once those tremors started, the only way to stop them was to sink into the hot tub. Heat on my skin didn't make up for the loss of his touch, but it was all I could find even faintly soothing. After the better part of an hour, I'd lie down again for another spin on the cycle. I slumped in our hot tub several times every night, trying to lift myself out of my head. *Transcend, transcend.* I'd glimpsed it before—that higher plane where this creature called Joni was a detail only, a fraction of the Everything that mattered. Where was that spiraling light of my vision, the sense that my soul could laugh gently at me and any torment I might feel? That place was peaceful and knew all was well. If only I could get there again.

Until Tony died, I had never tried to find or recreate that over-my-own-shoulder perspective. I'd honored the skull and crossbones that had arisen when I'd asked about a return. In the nights and days immediately after his death, my intentional efforts to get there all failed. Meditation, desperation, exhaustion, the endorphins of long-distance running—nothing worked. Now that I yearned for that vision of light, the assurance that my love's energy still flowed on, shining, I couldn't reach it. It danced in my memory but without soothing my heart. Without renewing the perspective that my grief here was unneeded. Without feeding my hope our two strands remained tightly entwined.

Yet I did get a confirmation of sorts, a reminder of my note that said, DO NOT DOUBT. About a year after Tony left, I received an unexpected gift from a close friend. I haven't known Monica long, but she has served as a compass rose through my grief. Her package held a spiral-y bracelet of multicolored strands. This wouldn't be remarkable by itself, but it arrived in my mail and I opened it two hours before a blog post about the spiraling light of my vision went live. Before she or anyone else could have read it. A consolation prize from the Universe, it was a souvenir of somewhere I'd been but apparently could not revisit.

As hard as I tried to reach that cosmic perspective, to transcend the pain of Tony's absence as temporary, I came close only once. Without trying. Not long after he left, I was driving his truck with the radio tuned to The Blend. "Like I'm Gonna Lose You" came on. Euphoria poured through me, a rush of gratitude for the mere gift of knowing and loving him. My joy was unadulterated by loss or dismay. Huge, it seemed to rise from beyond my body, the emotion of my much wiser soul shining through. Smiling broadly, I leaned into the seat as if into his chest. My hands caressed the steering wheel where his had gripped it and seemed to be gripping it right then through mine. Not merely peace but elation, this happiness lingered for miles.

An evening or two later found me wailing in our bed. Looking back, I couldn't relate to that transcendent joy, let alone recapture it. *Gone. He was gone.* My soulmate was dead. Gratitude continued to serve as my anchor, but joy became alien, lost with him. Was my elation that day obscenely belated because the truth of the loss had still not hit me yet? It could have been a habit almost, a reprise of the usual happiness that had always risen when I thought of our love. Or had the uber-Joni of my vision, who'd answered cosmic questions so long ago, stepped up briefly to console me before fading behind that one-way mirror again?

Not knowing might be the hardest part.

Mass Without Meaning

As midnight approached, I sat in an Ohio driveway belonging to Tony's oldest sister. I'd expected the sound of my rental car to bring his family rushing outside. Nobody did. My palms slid on the steering wheel's nubby plastic. The night held its breath while I tried to steel myself. But you can't prepare for such an arrival. You can only watch yourself act, knowing the weight of these actions, the momentous pivots they represent in your life. Not only is there no going back, the tipping point looms behind you—if it ever existed.

Earlier that week, on a day too painful to remain in my body, I had picked up Tony's ashes. While I floated two feet outside of myself, my reflexes apparently drove and signed paperwork, propped up by a soul sister who kept me upright. Brenda shuttled me to and from the Unnecessarily Far Away Mortuary chosen by Tony's oldest brother, the executor named in his outdated will. Then she nursed me with tea once back at her house to ground me for the remaining distance I had to go. When I climbed into Tony's truck to bring his ashes home, I realized that for the first time, I sat in his spot while he rested in my rightful place. I patted the box and smiled with him about that bittersweet switch.

Now I faced delivering those ashes to his family. As usual, he'd had more trouble than I did getting through airport security. We'd shared a psychic laugh about that.

I was not laughing now, but I clung to an incident at the airport that had made me feel Tony was with me. My shuttle bus had left me alone in the dark with three suitcases full of his family photos, his kids' mementos, and his ashes. A crosswalk, an escalator, and a long overpass stood between me and luggage check-in. Any two of the three bags outweighed me, and on the deserted curb, I couldn't ask for help. Except of one person.

"Ugh, sweetheart, I didn't think." Talking aloud to myself is a lifelong habit, but now I talked directly to him, never pausing to question that impulse. The Hershey's Special bars seemed evidence that he might answer. "How am I going to get all these inside to the check-in?" Leaving one there while I hauled the others upstairs would tempt thieves or TSA confiscation. With such irreplaceable contents, I didn't dare. Our airport has luggage carts near the baggage carousels but charges for them, so they're hard to come by except for the racks where they're locked up—inside. Besides, I stood in departures, outside. Even getting a cart would require leaving the bags. If I stood here long enough, would another shuttle bring more late travelers who might give me a hand? No headlights approached the entrance reserved for shuttles. The airport was unusually deserted.

Stymied, I turned in the other direction. Ten feet away stood an abandoned luggage cart, overlooked by the homeless folks who routinely work that gig, returning them for the deposit. As always, Tony helped with my bags.

Comforted by that auspicious start to the evening, I got out of the rental car and retrieved my carry-on from the backseat. Its cargo felt precious even though I find an attachment to ashes misguided. The medical examiner, before taking Tony's body away, had asked, "Would you like a moment with him?"

I'd shaken my head without looking again at his body. "That's just a shell," I replied. "He's already gone." Later a question would occasionally shove into my thoughts—had my gut instinct been right? Should I have held his hand, stretched out on the floor alongside him, pressed my lips to his one last time? Each time I've entertained this question, the specter of his pale, still body has risen before me and I'm glad that was not our last contact.

Still, I knew his ashes mattered to his family, just one of the reasons I'd brought them myself.

Calm, if a bit out of my body, I stepped up to the door. My knocking fist didn't reach it. When it unexpectedly opened, his sister-in-law behind it, I fell into her arms, instantly losing my calm into weeping at the sight of her face. Several hugs later, I was zipping my suitcase open in the entry, unable to discharge my duty fast enough. Three of Tony's four siblings were there, with two of their spouses. His daughter and son-in-law had arrived earlier and were sleeping nearby with his niece. The rest of us sat up into the wee hours, me perched on a fireplace hearth where I'd sat beside Tony, while I told them the details of his final hour. His sister's old dog gave me what comfort she could.

Three hard, hard days passed there. Being with eight members of his family without him and lying sleepless in a guest bed we'd shared was torture. Home had been bad enough, restless. No matter where I was, in our house or away, I wanted to leave as soon as I arrived. Movement promised relief but didn't deliver. The discomfort inside me could not be escaped. I spent hours wandering that Ohio neighborhood's icy sidewalks with my hoodie over my head to hide everything but the flat gray concrete rolling away under my feet. Simple and mesmerizing, it anesthetized me. Tony's siblings are warm, we'd stayed at the house twice before, and they embraced me as well as they could. His sister Lynn and I shared an unfortunate bond of grief, and I'm grateful for what she told me about losing her son. She also had an unexplained puzzle, like my Hershey's bars, which she held onto as a possible last hail from him. Still, it hurt to read the obituary his siblings had published without even running it past me. I kept my mouth shut about facts it got wrong and tried not to be hurt that it did not mention me.

A sigh also escaped me when I learned I wouldn't have the slightest say in the service they'd planned, let alone any role. By the time I arrived, the plans were complete, which should've occurred to me sooner. When I asked whether I might be allowed to speak, I was told Catholic funerals don't work like that. No wonder the Irish needed wakes. Speaking probably would have dissolved me into tears anyway, but a chance to try, to express my great love and respect, didn't seem like too much to ask. As it was, I felt like the owner of a human-remains courier service.

The morning we drove to attend the funeral Mass, the priest was so militant about allowing only family into the sanctuary first that I held back, uncertain. Did lovers count? Not to the Catholic Church. But Tony's brother took my arm and drew me in, making sure I sat with them. That kindness helped make up for the obituary.

The service was surreal. The whole event was surreal, filled with wild swings of emotion. In the narthex before we even began, I held back tears when I saw the photos displayed by his daughter. She'd sat on the floor at Lynn's house for hours, arranging her selections on big poster boards. Most of the images I had provided, hauling them in luggage, on thumb drives, on a laptop, but the display didn't include a single shot of us together. I contented myself that she used several I'd taken of her father clowning around underwater and on our backpacking trips.

Tony's son arrived with a new girlfriend who later became his wife. It relieved me to meet her and know he had support. Tony had worried most about him. Both his son and daughter were suffering, and not only because they'd recently said a final good-bye to their mom, too. Tony had been their emotional and financial foundation—understandably overprotective—for years. I hoped reaching out through our mutual loss might bring the three of us closer. Maybe we could share our respective memories, and they could feel they had an ally, if not a friend.

They weren't much interested, though. In our exchanges, which only happened on my initiative, they were considerate but not eager. Ultimately silence descended between us again. I understand. I suspect my name reminds them of too much—and not only their mother's decline, without which they'd never have met me. I was also the person with him when he died and a focus of the last years of his life. I wouldn't blame them for coveting that time and attention or simply wanting to forget I existed.

As we awaited Tony's Mass together, they were teary but cordial. We shared hugs and tissues, all still in shock, like well-dressed paper dolls of ourselves. The unexpected arrival of one of Tony's work colleagues and his wife added a dimension for me. Tony and I had shared meals with Jeff and Marie, and I'd spent most of an afternoon with Marie, showing her our Springfield house before Tony bought it. They'd known him for years, but they also knew the man he'd been with me recently. Standing on the cold tile floor and talking with them, my feet ached to protest such an event, but their presence helped me feel less like an interloper.

As we all walked into the chilly, flat air of the sanctuary, I winced at the butt-ugly red urn on display. Whoever had selected it must not have known its garish design was far too ornate for him. Regardless, I looked away quickly. His ashes had been mixed with Lynetta's, and while I doubt that decision was meant to rebuff me, that's how it felt.

Then came outrage as the priest mispronounced Tony's last name. Beside me, Lynn flinched. Later, the priest's overacting drew a giggle I had to suppress. With wild white hair, he looked like an ordained Donald Sutherland villain. I imagined an elbow from Tony beside me. The priest nearly redeemed his mispronunciation when he referred to my photos and thundered, "Look at those photos! He traveled the world! He may have gone to you too early, oh Lord—but he *lived*!"

To my mild surprise, both Tony's older brother and his nephew-in-law rose for readings. I longed for their places. Maybe not being Catholic disqualified me. Oh well. I buried my resentment in post-service conversation with Tony's dearest friends, Dennis and Mamie, who'd made the trip from Florida despite grueling health issues. I'd come to know and enjoy them over a half-dozen weekend visits we'd made to see them. Despite their own deep grief, they saw me. They knew how close we had been and weren't bound by blood to focus on his adult kids, so they spared me more concern than I'd felt otherwise. We comforted each other as equals.

Relieved to have this horrible milestone over, I escaped to the airport. I'd scheduled the close timing with purpose. The ragged hole in my life was smaller away from his siblings, whose own rips confirmed and expanded mine. Alone in my rental car, I felt Tony's presence more than I had in the church. The vapor of love around me was subtle, and I'd already realized I could best feel it alone.

It would be a long time before my own ritual did for me what that Catholic Mass was designed for.

Gods of Time

Time lost meaning, and so did my life. But one of the Bible readings from Tony's service stuck with me like a burr in my sock—the well-known verse of Ecclesiastes 3:1 that begins, in the King James Bible and the Catholic Bible used in the service, "To everything there is a season, and a time for every matter under heaven: A time to be born, a time to die; a time to sow and a time to reap. . . ." In English this verse emphasizes pendulum swings, and it's hauled out to encourage us to bear whatever comes because the opposite is sure to come, too. Its context is more pessimistic. The book's overall message emphasizes that earthly strivings are meaningless, so "man hath no better thing under the sun than to eat, and to drink, and to be merry. . . ." (Ecc 8:15)

Quibbling with Bible translations became a minor hobby of mine years ago after I discovered *Asimov's Guide to the Bible* by the science fiction author, who was Jewish and whose work traces the twists Christianity put on his native faith. Once home, fleeing my heart to shelter in the dusty bookshelves of my head, I looked up the funeral verse from Ecclesiastes. The Greek translation from the Hebrew uses *kairos* for what we now render "a time to."

The Greeks had multiple words for time. *Chronos* evolved into English words like chronological, the everyday concept of hours and minutes that march neatly in rows until time chews us up. The personified Chronos, like the Roman god Saturn, was a monster who ate his own kids.

Kairos is a rare moment, an opportune chance, a possibility that ought to be seized. *Kairos* changes fates. "Timely" is our best English equivalent. In statues that personified Kairos, winged feet made him fleeting. He carried a razor—the sharp edge of opportunities and decisions—and a scale to symbolize tipping points. His only hair was long bangs flying forward to be seized by whoever he approached. The back of his head was bald, because once he was past, there was no grabbing him. *Kairos* is about recognizing a chance. Its sense of inspired leaps and destiny-making is spiritual. Tony and I became acolytes of Kairos when we leapt into romance, and our reward came when our Ohio house sold overnight.

Kairos is the opposite of cycling seasons. As more recent versions of the Bible such as the New American Standard acknowledge, a richer and more accurate rendition of that verse in Ecclesiastes is, "There is *an appointed time* for everything, and *an appointed time* for every purpose under heaven." An appointed time to be born, an appointed time to die. An appointed time to get, and an appointed time to lose. A translation employing the full sense of both *kairos* and the Hebrew word before it defies the idea that everything comes around eventually. It more strongly implies a grand plan, an idea that better comforts even an infidel like me, one resistant to calling Tony's death "timely."

In their words for time, the Greeks also had Aion, the god of eternity and the afterlife. Once Kairos dictated the moment of Tony's death, when each of my days became eons long, it was Aion I was forced to consider. If not supplicate: *Please give me more glimpses into your afterlife realm.*

Two Hearts, One Body

"We're like the same person in two different bodies." Whatever prompted this comment from Tony has been lost in my memory, but it was probably a mundane suggestion like going out to the Rainier Grill for dinner that evening. In our few years together we'd honed our "shared glance" communication; we rarely had to speak to know what the other was thinking. It probably helped that we shared so many tastes, like having no use for TV other than football.

Even if he didn't mean it in any deep way, I treasured that comment. It captured my feelings when we were together, moving through and experiencing the world as one. Plus I don't think most men would admit they identified quite that much with a woman, no matter how much they loved her.

Secure in his masculinity, Tony never showed the slightest concern for what anyone else thought about it. No matter where we were, if my hands got full or I set it down briefly, he'd sling my purse over his shoulder like his own. The chivalrous gesture always made me giggle at this big-shouldered man with his fashion accessory. Endearing.

After he left, we became two different people in the same body—mine. As days passed, I latched onto short, soothing mantras. The first was "Both our hearts are beating now in my chest." I embodied that as much as I could. His Ohio State sweatshirt, as big as a Hefty bag on me, draped me for days.

Our unity felt clearest to me in our bed, where we had most literally shared one body. Holding me tight, he'd once said, "I want to pull you right inside my chest." The feeling was mutual. Now, lying in the gentle hollow his weight had made in our mattress, I worked to sense him inside. Or invent that comfort if needed. My own pulse, as if doubled over with his, pounded so hard it frequently kept me awake. It often still does. The shift from feeling his heartbeat with my cheek against his chest to sensing only my own rips my soul, but it does remind me of his love inside me and the ways we still nest inside one another.

It took me a while to see one of those ways. For the first couple of months without him, I barely slept. As a science experiment, it was impressive—I wouldn't have thought I could function on so little sleep. But I didn't want to sleep soundly. In fact, I'd have been grateful to die and never wake up. Short of that I was scared both of nightmares and of awakenings—of that instant when consciousness picks up the traces and allows anguish, briefly forgotten in sleep, to crash back into my heart. For a while, being forced to shoulder Tony's absence once more each morning was even worse than dragging it around the rest of the day.

To dodge the strike of that realization, I scrambled out of bed the second I opened my eyes, regardless of the hour. Day or night. After Tony's retirement we'd become professional dozers, lolling in bed and sometimes playing for an hour or more. After he left, I leapt away from those memories. From quiet thinking. From grief. I couldn't lie there to gaze at our new knotty-pine ceiling. For nearly a year he'd worked on that dormer and the bathroom below it. He'd enjoyed its completion for less than two weeks.

Eventually my terror of lying awake faded. Through witching-hour gloom or the light of morning, I could stare at our vaulted ceiling while the knots in the pine gazed back. That ceiling, the gray bathroom tiles they sheltered, the adjoining loft I could glimpse through the doorway—these were Tony's body on this earth with me now. They buzzed with the energy of his hands and inspiration, cherished gifts of his calculations and sweat. Lying in his place in our bed in that room, I rested inside him and he inside me. We were two hearts in one body now, as well as one heart beating within two bodies, one of those made of wood.

This metaphor sometimes burst into sensation. Later that summer I surfaced barely from sleep, feeling his presence beneath and around me. With my back against his chest, I was lying both on and within him. We'd stacked ourselves like that once on the deck of a dive boat, conserving warmth against the spray in an icy wind. Like then, Tony's arms wrapped around me, holding me in place atop him, enfolding.

Half asleep, I mumbled, "Thank you for being here, sweetheart. But let me turn over and sleep on you this way." I flipped to my belly, my weight balanced on one hip and him, more like we'd so often snuggled together. I pressed my left palm and my face to his chest and instantly fell back asleep. *Remember this*, I thought as I sank.

When I woke in the morning, he was no longer there, but I could recall how tangible he'd felt beneath me, surrounding me like warm, swirling water. I could summon the weight of his embracing arms.

After my first visit to him in Kentucky, I had listened obsessively to a song called "Spanish Sahara" performed by Foals. I'd first heard it several years before, when they recorded it live for a Seattle radio station.

> *I'm the Fury in your head*
> *I'm the Fury in your bed*
> *I'm the ghost in the back of your head.*
> — "Spanish Sahara," Foals

I have no idea what the musicians intended with these lyrics, but once I'd spent time with Tony, they captured my inability to get him out of my mind. I downloaded the song and began singing it under my breath.

Once he was gone, its resonance grew. I felt inhabited by him in ways that were sometimes startling. For instance, I began wearing one of his muscle shirts to our gym so I could pretend we were still working out together. Unexpected glimpses of myself in the mirrors startled me when they seemed to reflect not my shoulders and biceps, but his.

Other hints of possession were more practical. Electricity scares me, but my unease with it served as a useful distraction in the first couple of weeks after he left. The last touches of our remodeling project awaited, and the missing mirror and towel hooks and shelving shouted too loudly that he also was not there. I hurried to hang the mirror and finish other details.

The most daunting was the thermostat for our bathroom's in-floor heating. It's nearly impossible to get contractors to our mountain community, especially for small jobs. Besides, paying for something Tony had expected to do salted the wound. The 220-volt circuit involved would do more than make me curse if I touched it live, but I couldn't bear to leave the chore undone, either. It'd be a horrible waste of the considerable effort Tony had made to install the cable under the tile. Without it, the floor and room would remain as chilled as my heart.

Several times I removed the device from its box to study it. And maybe inoculate myself against its dangers. I'd helped Tony fish wires, held the flashlight while he connected outlets, and previously replaced small light fixtures myself. Could I finish his work? I felt him urging me on.

As he always had when faced with new projects, I applied generous amounts of "how-to" from YouTube. One gray afternoon, I took my nerves in my fist, pulled out a flashlight, and threw every breaker in the house, to be sure. If I electrocuted myself, it might bring us back together. That was enough consolation for me to proceed.

My hands shook at first. What was left of my heart sat in my throat. Kneeling on the cold tile, I asked Tony aloud for his help. Then I held the flashlight in my teeth. My mind found a balance between the how-to steps I'd studied and listening at the back of my head for his voice. Feeling as though my hands were guided, I wrangled the stiff 220 wire out of the wall, removed the wire caps, and tested the line. No warning lights flashed on the circuit tester.

No reason to bail, then. My fingers darted to the tip of the wire and away as if they could move faster than electricity. To my mild surprise, the line really was dead. Blisters formed as I stripped its heavy insulation, but I managed to connect the various wires to the right screws on the thermostat. More than once. In the tight mounting space between the door frame and a closet, shifting the device to reach the next connection often sprang loose a wire I'd already anchored.

"Come on," I pleaded. With the wires, myself, Tony. My frustration was replaced by compassion—a warm flood of patience, as though from him.

I took up my needle-nose pliers again. At last I got the screws tight enough. All the wires stayed connected at once. *Hooray!*

Belay that cheer. The box wouldn't fit flush in its hole. The stiff line behind it wasn't positioned right. Or something. The thermostat wanted to protrude at least an inch from the wall like a sunflower on a stalk, and no shoving or tilting could force it into place.

I took the flashlight from my teeth and wiped off the accumulating slobber. Could some merciful contractor be lured to the house, probably for a hefty surcharge, if I explained my home improver had died? That should at least stop them from laughing before they fixed what was so nearly done.

Nope. Disconnect it, accordion the wire tighter into the wall, and do it again. He was more patient than I was.

"I could do that, I guess." I obeyed. The second try did the job, with the advantage of practice. What a pro might've handled in thirty minutes took me and my spirit advisor four hours, but when I flipped the breakers back on, no burst of sparks came, only obliging LCD digits.

"Woo-hoo, sweetheart! We did it! Thank you so much!" I smiled the whole time I patched the drywall around it.

Buoyed by the sense I had help, I decided to also fix the ceiling fan switch. It had worked when he had installed it. Days after he'd left, I'd walked into the bedroom and reached for the light switch. Because they were new, my hand hit the wrong one. The *crackle— pop!* and flash from the switch made me jump. It only echoed my exploding world. At least it wasn't the light, which I couldn't do without. Summer wouldn't arrive in my life now anyway. Why did I need a fan?

To make Tony's work whole again, that's why. The blackened parts of the old switch looked ominous, so I bought a new one. Strangely, its wiring seemed more complicated than the thermostat's, but the 110-volt wire was easier to handle, and the switch took only one attempt to install. The short didn't repeat itself as I feared.

And I didn't shock myself even once. I still can't believe I managed those tasks, but I'm grateful. Not for the heat or the cooling but for the strong sense that Tony was with me—and proud.

Similarly, he advised from the back of my head the first time I put our camper on our truck by myself, and he gave me ideas for solving home maintenance problems. I'm a long way from helpless, but "Oh, good idea!" kept springing from my lips in reaction to suggestions that felt squarely not mine. In addition to the quiet voice of my own heart, I sometimes caught whispers that seemed to be his.

Maybe because Tony dreaded such things, he's never appeared

as a stereotypical ghost—no whiffs of his scent, no movement or shadow in my peripheral vision. His voice echoes in my mind rather than from down the hall. Having joined the Source of all intuition, perhaps he's just lending his words and bass voice. But I prefer him as "the ghost in the back of my head." That reinforces my other impressions that his spirit sometimes superimposes with mine.

What Dogs Know

Our dogs seemed more attuned to Tony's absence than his spirit's occasional presence. His black lab mix, Bape, had drooped immediately. Tony's long absence the previous fall hadn't fazed him, but after his death, Bape moped on the dog bed for about ten days before starting to act like himself.

Jazz didn't seem to react much the first week. No surprise there. He'd been my dog for years before meeting Tony, and he always disdained the house to spend most time outdoors. Still, when Jazz finally responded, he shocked me. One evening my aloof, would-be wolf came in through the dog door, climbed up, and curled next to me on the couch.

"What are you doing in here?" I asked. Maybe he'd heard thunder I hadn't. Storms and fireworks were his only motivations for ever seeking refuge in the house. It comforted me to have him there beside me, however, and maybe he knew I needed it.

It happened again the next night. And the next. He spent an hour or two next to me every evening for three solid weeks. Three weeks! That was easily the most time he'd voluntarily spent indoors over the entire decade I'd had him.

Just as I got used to his new routine, he returned to more usual behavior. Then, as our first month without Tony was ending, I headed out to the woodshed, blinked, and stopped short. There was Jazz, curled in the rain shelter I'd asked Tony to build. The dog hated enclosed or small spaces, which was partly why he shunned the house, but we'd thought a lean-to might work to protect him from bad weather. Once the lean-to was done, I'd coaxed Jazz into it twice, but he'd skulked out again the instant I let him. In the eighteen months since, he'd never set a paw inside that I knew. So spotting him there was even more startling than his coming indoors. In disbelief, I took a photo to give myself proof.

Two or three more times, and never during a rain, I stepped outside to find the dog in the house Tony had built. It must've been the dog's way of mourning his alpha male.

Jazz didn't go inside it again.

Talk to me all you want about the dogs reacting to a sudden absence and my often apparent distress. I wouldn't argue. Jazz's behavior still convinced me that dogs know more than we credit them for. We could probably learn from their attention to subtle forces.

In particular, the short time they mourn offers comfort. I don't believe it's because their memories are weak. There's evidence they know littermates years down the road.

Besides, if dogs' memories were short, Jazz wouldn't have remembered who built that lean-to. I'd rather believe they don't mourn very long because they have a clearer sense than we do of deeper connections or even a spiritual plane beyond this one.

Feelings 101,
Expression 102

Over the decades I've come to believe that if life is indeed a soul school, then I'm here to bone up on emotion: Feelings 101, Expression 102. Emotional intelligence has been one of my Achilles' heels, a weakness big enough to be an Achilles-sized foot. By the time I met Tony, I'd been working on it, but it still took me the entire week of that dive trip to admit my attraction to him. After that, every risk was rewarded. Honest, vulnerable communication became a self-reinforcing cycle. The emotional expression between us was so rich that he might've been my prize for graduating from Soul Grammar School. Yet surely I haven't progressed further than that.

When Tony left, my tough middle-school soul lessons started. My life had been shattered for only a few hours that first morning before I opened my laptop to answer email. Apparently many grieving people take time off from work. I can't understand why they'd want to. Lifting my brain from the ocean of tears to dry out for a few hours a day was the only thing that kept me from drowning. There was crying enough all the rest of the time. But how quickly the Universe slapped down my inclination to numb my heart with logistics and obligations!

The first email I sent that morning went to two friends, not because they were friends but because they were fellow volunteers with our writing organization. I told them Tony had stopped breathing and left me that morning, so I probably wasn't going to make an event in three days that I'd been responsible for. Would one of them pick up the workload for me by managing the last-minute confirmations and introducing the speaker?

One of those pals, Laurie, texted that she and her husband, Bernie, were on their way over. She knows me well enough, I guess, not to ask, not to give me the chance to dissuade her. It had never occurred to me that friends might come over, not with the hour-plus of travel required. Touched, I realized this nudge was a lesson. I need to seek less refuge in work and more in connections with other people. Even if my most-trusted person is gone. My heart, accustomed to being heeded, and swollen three sizes by love as a result, wouldn't survive stuffed in a file folder.

Laurie and Bernie spent several hours sitting with me. Only two memories of their visit stuck. I showed off Tony's remodeling work, and we recalled a recent dinner the four of us shared. Once Tony and I had found the restaurant, after walking past it twice in the rain, we all had a damp but delicious evening. Now we couldn't be "couple friends" after all.

In a way, that proved to be wrong. Spending time with them as a couple is hard, but it also summons the feeling of being coupled with Tony. He's there like an afterimage when I close my eyes. Plus Laurie, like many of my writing friends, is emotionally wise and a fantastic listener—the perfect kind of tutor for me. Others, like my fiber-arts buddy, Deb, have too much experience with grief of their own but have forged it into compassion they share. I try not to lean on any one of them too much; I can't risk wearing them out. I need them too much. I'm learning to bear getting weepy with them, if only because I can't help it, and my small handful of besties can let me do that without escaping to the bathroom. When not emotionally naked, we laugh, too. Most of them never even met Tony. That's a regret I would've fixed with more time. More of my friends should've had a chance to see for themselves how awesome he was. In addition to the logistical hurdles, however, I was coveting every moment we had for myself.

Now that I don't have a choice, I'm actively trying to learn my lessons. Emotional intimacy with friends is a hard class for me, and I'm not sure what's in it for them. But my heart keeps muttering to finish my homework, and I know it's important because Tony himself made a visit to tell me.

Packing My Bags

Tony's ghostly embrace in the twilight between waking and sleep, the one where I turned to press my face into him, was my first experience that felt like a visitation. Months passed before I had another. But the stress-relief supplement Laurie shoved into my hands the next time we met reintroduced me to sleep. Eventually I could stay down five or six hours a night. The nightmares I'd dreaded, replays of our CPR session, never came. Four months and one day after Tony left, I had that first special dream.

We were preparing to travel somewhere, but for some reason we had to take different flights. That didn't seem strange. We'd taken different flights back from Palau, too, not to mention the times he'd visited his son without me. I knew we'd get to the same place once the traveling was done.

His flight left first, but not before I gave him a long hug—so sweet, holding him, my face on his chest, not only pressed close but blurring together. We merged at the edges. Then he stepped back and faded into the dark.

Right, then: I had to finish my packing. I turned to my suitcase, open on the bed. It seemed full already. What else did I need? Oh, here was a swimsuit to go in. But wait—hadn't I put that in already? I dug through what I'd already packed in the bag, having trouble recognizing what was there and wasn't.

Time was short now. I had to hurry! I didn't want to miss my flight and my connection with Tony. Scrambling, I made a hash of my suit-case. *Shit.* With no idea what I'd packed and what was still missing, I had to dump it back out and start over. *Hurry.*

I woke up, immensely grateful for our hug, which felt like a visitation, and for the reassurance we'd be reunited—after I finished something I had to do and our "traveling" in this life was done. This is Dream Interpretation 101, a course I've already passed. Except for my confusion with what I was packing. Haven't I stuffed in the important contents already?

Apparently not. I'm not certain what I still have to do on this earth that's so vital, but I have a good guess. Tony gave me a hard time for being too independent. After more than ten years alone, I knew no other option. But he and I fell so easily into divided labor, all those miniature ways to make love to each other, from my cooking for him to his washing my car. Never in my life had I been so domestic, and I'd just gotten used to him carrying my suitcase. It was a mean trick for him to leave me just as I got comfortable depending on him. After so many years as a point of pride, doing everything myself has become a punishment. Nonetheless, it's pushing me to learn to ask for more help. That's one item still missing from my suitcase, I guess, and part of building more intimate connections with friends. The course catalog probably calls it Remedial Interdependence. I'm trying to apply what our relationship taught me to rely on and share emotions with someone other than him.

Four or five people are helping with this. The two most patient, helpful, wonderful friends are two people I never would have expected to become so important. From the background of my life they emerged suddenly like porters offering to help me with my psychic bags. If saints moonlight as porters, that is. It's true that losses reveal who your real friends are.

Grief for Emotional Dummies

In addition to the life lessons I'm trying to learn, I found myself enrolled in a crash course I didn't want called American Incompetence with Death and Grieving.

Our society insists on dismissing our hearts' valid feelings, especially when it comes to things we want to deny. Death tops the list. It's not a shared and inevitable burden; it's an unexpected bump we need to "get over." Preferably by flipping a switch. Like the switch on the cheap plastic tea lights handed out by the leader of a grief group I attended.

"Lighting the flame honors your person," she explained. (Don't get me started on the frequent use of "your person," as if we were all dogs or cats, instead of "your loved one," which applies for anyone wounded enough to seek grief therapy.) She turned over a fake candle to demonstrate.

"Could we bring in our own real candle?" asked a widower. "My wife loved candles. I'd like to bring one of hers."

So sorry, but no open flames in the building. Flick on your fake candle at the start of the session. Flick it off at the end. Thanks for returning them neatly to their box.

No, there's no metaphor here.

Even when not asked to stuff infernos of love and grief into a thirty-cent LED, the bereaved endure so many thoughtless comments that poke the wound by belittling it. Here's a tip from Joni's Big Book of Grief for Emotional Dummies: Losing a partner is not like losing your cat. I've grieved many beloved dogs; please take my word for it. And no, it isn't much like divorce, either. My divorce parted me from my husband, my best friend, and my home. To make a long story short, the three of us embarked on an ambitious threesome just as polyamory joined the vocabulary of talk shows. My motives were to make both of them happier while buying free time for interests my husband didn't share but made him sulk if I tried to pursue them without him. I loved both people enough to make it work—for a while. After several years and a real estate purchase together, my friend's jealousy of me became too much to bear. It seemed richly ironic, given what I'd considered a generous arrangement. Telling them I could no longer do it, I found myself voted off the island after weeks of my husband's indecision and several reversals. Though only my heaven-sent romance with Tony helped me forgive any of us, including myself, I've always been grateful for our experience, too. They taught me a shitload about love, human nature, and pain.

And the implosion of that relationship was a lollapalooza alongside Tony's death. Comparing even such a messy divorce to his loss is like comparing a grenade to a nuclear bomb.

At least missteps like that come from well-meaning people trying to say, "I'm sorry. That hurts, and I get it." They don't, but that doesn't negate their compassion. Equally stupid things probably fell from my lips, too, after friends lost pregnancies or a parent but before I learned the hard way. Since we generally refuse to talk with kids about death, we simply don't know until we wish we didn't. Besides, we're all different. What pisses me off might comfort someone else who is grieving. Exhibit A: plastic tea lights. I was the only one in the group who politely declined.

Others say things harder to cast as well-meaning. Welcome to my Most Punchable Well-Wisher Award! We have three nominees:

The Nominee for Most Inept Change of Subject Within the First Month: "So what else is new?" What response did the two friends who asked this expect? "You should see the cute outfit I wore to the funeral!" or maybe, "Now I get mail addressed to someone dead. That's fun!"

The Nominee for Most Confused: "They just don't live long enough, do they?" Wha—? *Men don't? Lovers don't? Plenty of others seem to!* By the time I realized this poor listener thought I'd lost a pet, it wasn't worth setting her straight.

The Nominee for Most Heartless Friend: "Now you have experience with dead bodies." Fighting a "fuck you," I took a deep breath. Maybe I could turn this exchange into an opportunity for communication that might strengthen the friendship. "Ouch," I responded. "That makes me want to swear at you." His reply showed me the relationship didn't even rate a Darwin Award.

Most friends, of course, managed admirably, and a handful of relationships are closer as a result. Still, if Tony has afterlife superpowers, I hope he'll tell people to stop asking, "How are you?" Don't ask. There's no way to answer. "Terrible, thanks for asking," is already taken. (It's the title of a great podcast I recommend.) I despise telling people, "I'm okay" when I'm not. I won't be. Stop expecting me to. I can let y'all know if or when that ever changes. Even the people who care most can't help, not as much as they'd like, so there's no point in saying, "Suicidal, thanks. You?" Honesty spotlights how helpless we are, which is probably why we're so reluctant to engage with the truth. But following my instincts into Tony's arms taught me more respect for my heart. I refuse to throw my inner truth under the bus to protect others' comfort.

Since I'm not a sadist, however, I experimented with inscrutable answers: "Today I feel taupe." "Eh. It's a fuzzy elephant day." Sometimes I threw out a random number like three without mentioning that the scale went to one hundred, not ten. Predictably, this confused people when the last thing I wanted to do was explain. My best answer became, "I haven't shot anyone." It's true, it sounds like a joke, and it's timely, given our country's affection for Mass Shootings of the Day. No one catches that the "anyone" I mean is me.

When I'm feeling less perky, I don't answer at all, but I'd rather never hear the question again. It's stupid, nothing more than a reflex. We might as well bark a greeting like dogs. Friends can launch directly into more meaningful conversation. Strangers don't care anyway.

One of the terribly small dividends of losing Tony, however, is that it's helped me feel even closer to him because I can better relate to his grief over Lynetta—and to the harmful reactions of others, including avoidance and a false pretense that nothing has changed. I realize now how that pain must've weighed inside him, even when he was laughing and smiling with me. I know firsthand how work offers a dead-end escape and what it's like to lie awake at night weeping, as he admitted he had. Though I'm sure I sob harder and with less chance of anyone hearing.

Grief is another way we've become superimposed. It has eliminated a border between us that used to be enforced mostly by skin. Meanwhile, its lessons keep coming, providing plenty of material for Joni's Big Book.

Getting Real

Our real estate agent in Ohio showed me a better way to help friends facing grief. Her prize-winning performance has become my model for honoring broken hearts.

Sheila and I had great fun touring houses, and I valued her warmth and wisdom. It pleased me to get her another commission when we sold the house, too, but I never expected to hear from her after we moved away.

A week or so after Tony had gone, my phone rang: Sheila. Half expecting a butt dial, I answered.

"I heard about that sweet man of yours through the plant grapevine!" she exclaimed, referring to the Navistar plant Tony had led. "I was so sorry to hear it!"

She recalled seeing us holding hands at a festival in Snyder Park weeks before we had moved. "You were so into each other, you weren't noticing me. But it was obvious how pure your love was. It shone out of you both every time I saw you."

She'd lost a brother she'd mentioned while driving me around between showings. That's probably how she knew what to say. She reflected our relationship back to me, like a mirror, and reminded me of a moment of joy. That call was priceless. Only my mother, who'd expressed her sorrow by saying, "You were like two halves of a whole!" gave me equal comfort. The key in both cases was validation: of the rare connection we'd had, of the magnitude of the loss.

Sheila also spoke for the Universe in a way she couldn't have known. Before our call ended, she told me the man who had purchased our house had been transferred at work, vacated the house, and put it back on the market just a few months after we left. At the time of her call, it was still sitting empty. Before we bought that house, I had shared my Real Estate Kismet theory with her. Sheila laughed, saying, "You've probably got a healthy attitude there." Hearing the quick sale that had freed us from Ohio had flipped—without improvements— into another listing merely strengthened my conviction.

Since then, my Internet snooping revealed that First Alferio National only recently sold for 15 percent less than Tony received and after languishing for more than two years—the timeframe we'd originally anticipated. The neglect of a house we filled with love saddens me, but I count our speedy sale as divine intervention and a confirmation of my intuition. The Universe and I both knew Tony's time was short so we needed to get back to my Northwest home.

Sheila ended our phone call by saying, "He was a good man you had. I'm so sorry you didn't have him for longer." It seems ironic that someone I barely knew gave me so much more comfort than several closer connections. She taught me a more helpful way to support someone in grief than a generic condolence like "I'm sorry for your loss."

The trouble is this line sounds like cheap tuna—canned. Our preferred words for apology simply don't fit. My initial reaction is always, *Well, it isn't your fault.* "I'm sorry," is a deeply conditioned reaction, especially for women, but couldn't be more generic. "That really sucks," conveys more honest feeling to me. It would probably strike plenty of others as crude or dismissive. More genteel but still accurate expressions include, "I wish this hadn't happened," or "I ache for the pain you must feel." Or "The challenges of agency within our existential position in the multiverse are daunting, aren't they?" if you console many college professors.

That said, bland regrets are better than clip-art platitudes. "They're in a better place," and "It was their time," and anything that begins, "At least . . ." and all those other rote phrases that spring to mind when we're speechless hurt more than they help. They're backhanded ways to say, "This topic makes me uncomfortable. Please stop feeling bad so I won't have to, either. What else is new?"

Okay. Rant over. I'm not without sympathy for the narrow plank that bystanders (me among them) must walk. We're not all Interpersonal Gurus like Sheila. A lot of us balance precariously between the empathy-free "It was Some Deity's plan" and the indulgent pity—if not outright disdain—contemporary Western culture bestows on any faith in an afterlife. Despite research that consistently shows up to 80 percent of Americans believe in life after death, we're still so wedded to scientific reductionism that many people are reluctant to admit it, let alone raise the topic while the Reaper's still in the room.

My own faith in an afterlife is shaky, I admit, despite numinous experiences over my life. My faith in science is pretty strong, too, and the Church of White Lab Coats declares an afterlife not merely hard to test but heretical. Science has taken a long time to admit its own gospel might be less than divine. It has a replication crisis, for starters, because human weaknesses and politics influence findings, not to mention which questions are deemed worth asking.

When I think deeply about the tension between my two brands of faith, I realize this, too, began with my sister's death.

Guilt

Although the flu was the nominal cause of Jo Anna's death, there's more to the story than that. My earliest memory is a glimpse of her standing in her crib with an orange stuffed dog that was mine. Outrage over private property rights is surely why that scene stuck in my three-year-old brain.

My next memory comes from the day of her death. I would have sworn on my own grave that Mom was behind our duplex unit that morning, hanging laundry on the line.

"No," insists my mother. "No, no, no. That's not right, Joni."

She and I are sitting at a mall café table. I'm in my thirties. We have never discussed this before. Already, from the start, her memory is different.

We tussle a moment, but I give in to her version. Her memory is probably not trustworthy either, but hers is more reliable than mine. More robust, too. She knows, for instance, that my dad had been working nights, returning home about 3:00 a.m.

"I was trying to keep you kids quiet during the day while he slept and then staying up half the night with him too." She swallows hard. "I was tired. I got in the habit of napping with him when he came home and crawled into bed every morning. I usually woke a few hours later when you did and caught up with you as you helped Jo Anna from her crib or pulled out the Cheerios box for you both. You were so independent and such a good sister. I didn't think I could sleep through the two of you getting up." My memory of her being outside with laundry must have been either an incorrect toddler assumption or another memory superimposed over this one. Or both.

After an uneven breath, my mother goes on. "But that morning I did. I made a terrible mistake. So what happened was my fault. Not yours."

I don't agree with her conclusion but don't bother to argue whose fault it was. I know it was mine. My memories of the events and my involvement are clear. I went into the bathroom and climbed onto the closed lid of the toilet. From there I could reach the sink faucet.

And the medicine cabinet. I got out two bottles, white pills and tiny orange ones. If I shook the bottles, they rattled. We could make music.

Jo Anna's blond wisps didn't reach the counter, but I was a good sister. I gave her a shake-bottle, too. One for her, one for me.

Two years before the invention of childproof caps, I discovered I could open the bottles.

Jo Anna had a spoon in her fist. She liked to bang it on the counter. And on orange and white pills. We smashed some and crunched more between our new teeth. It sounded fun to make soup, adding water from the faucet to crumbs in the spoon. The bottle caps worked as bowls, too. The orange pills tasted better but the white looked like milk. I fed the baby. I fed her and me.

My next memory is terror: *Strangers!* Strangers surround me, tall ones in white coats. A strange metal bed holds me, and I can't get out. The walls are an unpleasant olive-green and nothing in this room looks like a house. *Mom! Dad! Where are you? What's happening to me?*

Doctors were pumping my stomach, that's what. I survived our aspirin overdose. Jo Anna didn't. My parents didn't even realize aspirin was involved until they returned from the hospital and found the bottles.

On the fine points, my memory combats with Mom's. "You kids did get the aspirin." Tears clog her voice as she says this. "Because I stupidly left it out on the counter." She describes how sick Jo Anna and I both had been with the flu and adds, "When I got the baby aspirin and gave you each one, the cap fell into the sink and got wet, so instead of putting it back onto the bottle, I left the bottle on the edge of the sink and the cap by it to dry. I didn't think you could reach it. Your little hands were so quick, though! Your dad and I used to joke that you'd grow up to pick pockets. I should have hidden it away somewhere safe. And then, horribly, I forgot about it."

Nope. She may have been sleeping and not in the yard—our attempts since to reconcile our memories of that day still hold confusions and contradictions—but I distinctly remember how proud I was to reach the medicine cabinet and open it. *Joni a big girl now, Mom!* Perhaps the baby aspirin *was* on the counter, but the adult aspirin came from the medicine cabinet. The difference doesn't much matter. I would've gotten my hands on the bottles regardless.

Nevertheless, I don't argue. It's pointless. There in the mall, amid canned music and the chatter of shoppers, Mom stares at her knuckles. "Jo Anna woke us that morning. Your dad heard her first. She was making these horrible, horrible—" Her voice fails. She wipes the tears rimming her eyes and goes on. "She was making these choking noises. It terrified me. We grabbed up you and her, and your dad drove like a madman to Madigan [Hospital], horn blaring all the way as we ignored the red lights and swung around other cars on the road. She was . . . convulsing . . . so hard I could . . . barely hold her."

My mother is nearly convulsing now, too, trying to hold in her sobs. After blowing a few breaths through pursed lips, she continues. "We dashed in and the doctors snatched her away. The doctor in charge called your dad to his office . . . not us both, just your dad. Military protocol, I guess. When they called for me too, it was a long walk through the corridors. I thought Jo Anna was okay. That they'd admitted her to the ward and needed some paperwork. They took you from me without explanation before I went into the room where your dad waited."

She looks down at her untouched coffee on the table between us. "He was sitting there, crying." The doctor had already given Dad the bad news.

"The doctor said, 'Your little girl is gone.' Just like that." Mom's voice cracks. "I'm thinking, *Gone where*?! And I have two little girls! They must have us confused, they must have the wrong family!" Her hands knead together. "They wouldn't let us in to see you until later. They were trying to make sure that if you'd both gotten poison, it wouldn't kill you, too."

They didn't yet know what had killed the baby. My devastated parents told the doctors we'd both had the flu and how much we'd been vomiting in the days before Jo Anna's death. The resulting dehydration may have caused the convulsions. Mom recalls how my sister grasped at a glass of water to drain it in the hours before her convulsions began. But there's no way to know which problem was fatal and which only contributed to her death. Since they had no idea what the real issue might be, the doctors took every precaution they could with me. By then it was too late for my sister.

"We left the hospital dazed, held her funeral in shock, and never discussed what had happened," Mom said. "Not once. It seemed like it'd stir all the grief, all the guilt. This is really the first time I've ever talked about it all the way through."

I'm not surprised. My family kept the important things inside. Like blood, feelings and secrets were too frightening when they came out. My dad still won't really discuss Jo Anna.

"It isn't because your dad doesn't care," Mom told me. "He doesn't know how. He swallowed his grief and built a wall around Jo Anna's place in his heart. That seemed to be the only way he could deal with it. I was terrified that if I ever broke past that wall, he'd blame me for what lay behind it. So I never tried."

It disoriented me to hear my mother express the same fear of blame I'd felt for so long, fear that had silenced us both. Our conversation did not persuade me, however, that Jo Anna's death wasn't my fault. I'd already retrieved her death certificate from the county website. It confirmed my own memory that aspirin poisoning, not the flu, had killed her, exploding the story I'd heard as a kid. I knew where—and from whom—that aspirin had come.

The paramedics who questioned the aspirin bottle on our windowsill the morning of Tony's death had no idea how their suspicion had resonated.

Absolution

While I was still growing up, the wound of Jo Anna's death affected our whole family. My younger brother might be an exception, but he, too, was raised in an emotional climate I now recognize as less than ideal, at least by today's more enlightened standards. Don't get me wrong; my parents deserve cake, and my childhood was happy, but I come by my emotional idiocy naturally.

As a toddler, my memories of Jo Anna's last morning stuck with me. I didn't think about them deeply for six or eight years. Perhaps my brain and emotions hadn't developed enough. The official story had been that Jo Anna died of dehydration from the flu. Then in the early 1970s, Reye's Syndrome entered public awareness. In a rare conversation about my sister, Mom and I decided she'd been an undiagnosed victim at a time when baby aspirin—the little orange ones—was still an approved treatment for the flu. This brief conversation was the first acknowledgement I could recall that aspirin had even been involved.

Guilt began to haunt me. The aspirin consumed by Jo Anna had not been a pill now and then for a fever, and I assumed Mom knew what I recalled, too. That was part of our secret. When I thought no one would notice, I sneaked into our hall closet to pull out a particular scrapbook tucked in the back. This album, its cover embossed with silver scrollwork and text, was the baby book Mom had begun for Jo Anna. My brother and I each had one, too, and I occasionally enjoyed giggling at their contents. No laughter rose when I stole into my room with Jo Anna's, which was as pristine as if it were new.

On its first pages, my mother's handwriting curled, listing baby-shower presents and who gave them to her. Jo Anna's July birthdate struck me. So did the date of her death, four days after Christmas. Two more things I should know but didn't remember. What a terrible end to a holiday season to face over and over each year. Even her name made me blink when I saw it. She occupies one word in my mind: Joanna. Her middle name was Anna, but we'd always used both. Little Jo never got old enough to decide for herself.

A pale blonde twist, baby's first haircut, was wrapped in a fold of yellowing plastic, the tape holding it to the page brittle and losing its stick. One or two photos followed, including one that looked familiar, probably because I'd seen it before rather than because I remembered the situation. Two little girls sat on a blanket spread near the trunk of a tree at my grandparents' house. I would stare into the younger girl's eyes, wondering how my life might be different if I still had that sister.

There weren't many clues in the book. My mother's handwriting stopped within just a few pages. After that, a yellowed snip of news-paper lay caught in the book's gutter, looking like a classified ad. Its text was so curt, it would barely make sense if you didn't know what "entered into eternal rest" meant. It didn't say sweet things about her or invite readers to a memorial service. To this day I don't know if I attended a funeral or, more likely, was left home in somebody's care. This brief notice had been laminated by the funeral home, like a bookmark, though most of its length was clear plastic. It marked nothing in her book but silence.

If I made the mistake of turning the page, I regretted it. The next page was blank. And the next. And the next. No answers for prompts such as baby's favorite food, baby's first sentence, baby's best friend. So many preprinted questions, unanswered. Blank. Blank. Blank. They hit me in the face. The first time, I kept turning the thick pages, wrinkling my nose at the chalk smell of dust. I kept thinking Mom's handwriting might appear again, recording some memory or anguish or prayer. Tearstains, perhaps. A photo from film not developed for months. Jo Anna's baby book has more heft than mine or my brother's, a harder, more permanent cover, more pages of blank irony. But my sister's recorded history ended with an inch of newsprint.

Those blank pages made me want to scribble madly on them or grab scissors and cut them all out. A short book would've been better than one so incomplete. Its silver embossing glinted from the cover, a shining lie hiding those horrible blanks. Slipping out of my room, I stashed the book back in the closet until the next time I needed to reassure myself of the truth under my family's silence.

Belatedly I've realized that Jo Anna's scrapbook lurks beneath a more recent need—my urge to hide that second copy of the Shutterfly book where I documented the start of my romance with Tony. My sister's book became my only touchstone to her. Instinctively, I created a similar scrapbook for Tony, proof he'd existed for once he was gone. Proof nobody's silence could hush. Proof that could not be forgotten. In addition, immediately after he left, I began jotting random memories of him in a journal, everything from the way he pulled out his wallet to his favorite expressions. I haven't opened that journal since my last entry in it. Still, it comforts me to know that I can, because some memories are fading. That hurts. Fortunately, we made many intense ones together, and my adult mind has held them better than my toddler mind could.

I never dared to look through Jo Anna's book alongside my mother. There seemed no chance to ask things I'd wondered about: If I'd noticed Jo Anna wasn't with us when we left the hospital. Whether I'd cried when I realized she wouldn't be back. If I'd been to the services noted in her obituary. At some point in my twenties, Mom told me how she'd sobbed so much while my dad was at work that the neighbor in the other half of our duplex told her not to forget she had one little girl left. Even when my mother volunteered information like that, I never knew how to respond. I'd internalized the perhaps unintentional message that the subject brought pain, and I wanted to avoid any further transgression because I had no doubt Jo Anna's death was my fault.

For months, I lay sleepless at night, wondering how my parents could love one daughter who'd killed the other. Wiping tears on my pillow, I begged both them and her to forgive me. Jo Anna never appeared or replied, and slumber-party séances did not summon her. Eventually I wore out my guilt or succeeded in repressing it.

More importantly, I found a back door around it. Life had already shown me things were not as they seemed. Secrets and contradictions lay beneath every surface, from the Watergate scandal to the discovery that one of my aunts was a closeted lesbian. Science claimed to be factual but was not more transparent. Solid objects are mostly empty space, after all. The most immobile boulders are made of atoms that vibrate, and ice and invisible mists are both water.

Everything from Nancy Drew mysteries to decoder rings in cereal boxes suggested life's depths could be plumbed, if you tried. My vanished sister was not an exception. Nothing at Sunday school reassured me. Most of what I learned there was too abstract to be useful or so vague it seemed clear the teachers didn't know, either. Besides, I couldn't imagine an existence more boring than sitting on clouds surrounded by angels. How could any heaven be so unrewarding? The deeper answer had to be something else.

With talking about Jo Anna off limits, I turned to books. After reading my share of ghost stories, I moved on to books about reincarnation. Those resonated not only with my dream about jumping off a mountain but with a strange phase I went through in second grade. For a while I loved to pretend to be a wounded Civil War soldier "taken in" by a playmate who lived in the apartment upstairs. We decided her "husband" was fighting for the other side and might return home any moment to kill me. We only stopped when my play-mate's grandmother overheard us and made us play something else. Whether it struck her as violent or merely odd, she hadn't liked what she'd heard.

When I discovered stories of past lives, soulmates, and karma, I could not get enough. They didn't convince me, mostly because the stories seemed to contain too many reborn queens and artists and not enough peasants and slaves. It wasn't until my twenties and my own regression experience that my interest gained the emotional valence to catalyze a belief. Today I consider the recycling of souls more likely than not.

But before that, the possibility helped absolve my guilt. Maybe Jo Anna was already back here on Earth, happily living in some other family. Perhaps someday we'd meet. Would we know each other?

Reincarnation led me to ESP, premonitions, intuition, the col-lective unconscious. The Bermuda Triangle inspired a school report and I made a science fair exhibit on pyramid power. My experiment failed to prove my hypothesis but didn't discourage my exploration. It introduced me to mummies and the tantalizing title of *The Egyptian Book of the Dead*.

By the time I was thirteen, I couldn't understand opposition to abortion. What did it matter if a given baby wasn't born?

When I voiced that opinion, my mother said, "You're too young to be so cynical about life."

"I'm not cynical!" The label surprised me. "Those souls will get another chance in some other body." For better or worse, my guilt over Jo Anna's death had crystallized my worldview. My growing belief in a spiritual realm may have been little more than my adoles-cent defense mechanism.

The alternative, however, is not tenable for me. Mysticism got me through my remorse over Jo Anna, so that's where I turned when I lost Tony, too.

Everything I Do

My first summer without Tony was buoyed by comforts like the Hershey's Special bars I'd found, the notes of meaningful songs, dreams about packing my bags. When a big check I'd mailed to his executor went astray, I could snicker. Tony would've been mad that I had to pay his estate for his fourteen-year-old truck, the little camper we'd bought together, and thousands of dollars for some imaginary tax liability I knew would never materialize. Heck, I was mad, too, but not going to fuss. I didn't expect Tony to protest by waylaying my check! Those two weeks when it was "lost" in the mail made the point.

Ultimately, such synchronicities weren't enough. They're too ephemeral. As author Josh Hanagarne wrote in *The World's Strongest Librarian*, "The problem with epiphanies is that they can't sustain you forever." [1]

Days passed. I awoke in the morning and sighed: another day without Tony.

Another.

Another.

Still more, unsustained by his presence or signs or sweet dreams. Nights swung me over the void.

Fear is an underappreciated aspect of grief. I fought it by recording tiny memories I was afraid I'd forget, from the scar on Tony's forehead caused by a school football helmet to how he'd rested his chin on my head. Videos of us sledding helped me preserve his voice.

For advice I scoured every grief memoir ever written, among them Roger Rosenblatt's *Kayak Morning*, which ends, "Grief. The state of mind brought about when love, having lost to death, learns to breathe beside it. See also love."

Although I liked that, I wanted to modify it: Death breathes the same air as love from the start. We ignore their proximity, claiming love is blind, but I'd shot furtive glances at death during my whole time with Tony, trying not to be terrified by it.

Famous grief guy David Kessler suggests in his books and workshops that we try to remember with more love than pain. Our love overflowed; it should've been easy!

Boy, did I underestimate the pain. Friends and family members like to tell people in grief they're strong. I get it. When a friend's husband was diagnosed with a degenerative brain disease, I too marveled at how strong and competent she looked. News flash: We've got virtually no other choice. No matter how much I wish for a different result, to date I've woken up every morning. The body eventually demands toilets and picking up off the floor. Other people stuff food into you when you don't seek it yourself, and most of us care enough for the feelings of those around us to eventually answer phones, doors, and emails. We mow overgrown lawns and pay utility bills. Society frowns intensely on the alternatives.

Tony had been gone a bit over four months when I started telling him through my journal, "I don't know if I can do this."

Working hard to maintain our routines, I finished many workouts in the corner of our Anytime Fitness gym, nominally stretching and hiding my face so nobody spotted my tears. While on a stationary bike there, it struck me that whenever I did something we'd done together, and anything new we'd have tried as a team, it was a way of making love to him still.

Accepting that mission, I appreciated nature's beauty and light, letting Tony experience it through my eyes and ears. In that spirit, I tried to travel without him. He and I had booked a trip for September that the airlines would only partly refund. Trying to do what he'd want, I used our nonrefundable flight to hike the West Highland Way and hoped to feel him walking beside me in a country we'd been in together.

That proved excruciating. The airports and planes we'd so enjoyed together shouted his absence. Trains and sidewalks in Glasgow demanded to know what I was doing there by myself. His death loomed over Big Ben and Ben Nevin. Forget diving; I could barely manage walking without him. Underwater, I'd drown when I started to cry. At least once a day I considered bailing from Scotland, beating a path to an airport, and going back home.

Nonetheless, a strange highlight occurred halfway through my hike. One evening I stepped into a trailside pub, the only dinner choice in the village. A professional-looking blonde woman sat near a window, a drink on her table. Slightly younger than me, she wasn't dressed as a hiker. I noticed because it was rare to see anyone else, particularly a woman, alone. On the trail, yes, but not in the pubs. Solo guys usually clustered at the bar, chatting with the barkeep or each other. I have no idea where other lone female hikers ate, but in countless pub meals over the years, I've virtually always been the only single woman. The unwritten rule against loners in restaurants is apparently enforced in the rural British Isles.

Since the Pub Police haven't caught up with me yet, I ordered a cider and a goat cheese salad and settled in a cozy corner to read. My salad arrived, and I kept flipping e-pages—until I glanced up to notice the blonde woman still there. That seemed slightly odd. Her drink had been half-finished twenty or thirty minutes before, when I'd entered. Now she stared sadly out her window.

Unable to drag my gaze from her, I raised my iPad Mini and

pretended to keep reading to disguise my stare. She wiped a finger discreetly under one eye and looked down at her lap. She was mourning, too. I knew absolutely. A compulsion was born: I had to go talk to her.

I don't talk to people trapped alongside me on planes, I hate having to barter in markets, and I don't chat up locals, though all are considered key to a full travel experience. Approaching this stranger terrified me. But I *had* to. The words I should say began popping into my head.

Fighting the impulse, I picked at my salad while peeking at her. At last she put cash on the table and gathered her things.

An external force stood me up and walked me toward her, because otherwise it was going to be too late. I watched myself in horror. *I can't believe I'm doing this. She's going to think I'm rude, insane, or both.* As she stood up, I reached her and parroted the script in my head: "Forgive me if this is inappropriate, but you look sad, and I can relate. Did you lose someone?"

She gave me a startled look, almost certainly thinking, *Who the hell is this Yank and what kind of manners do they teach over there*? After a moment, she said, "Yes, I did. Have you?"

I was expecting the "yes," but not her question. My script hadn't prepared me for that. If she'd said, "Uh, no" or "Mind your own business" or any of a hundred things I hadn't considered, I would've apologized profusely while running away. But I had *known* she'd say yes. So I also replied, "Yes," and went back to my script: "Would you like to talk about it?"

She re-a-ll-y hesitated. I took two steps backward. "I'm sorry, I'll let you go," rose to my lips.

Before I could sound them, she said, "Why don't we?" She gestured to the chairs at her table.

She told me about her husband, whose Highland funeral she'd held nearby that afternoon, fifteen days after he'd died.

"I was having a dram in his honor." She told me how long they'd been married, how they'd come to this area as a compromise between his Inverness and her London, but now she'd probably go back to her London police job because they wanted her to, and she needed a job, and she wasn't sure what else to do. On and on, while we gripped each other's hands for comfort. (Strangers! In Scotland! In a pub!) I don't know when that hand-holding started, but her fingers were slender and pale and cool, her wedding ring made of platinum. She'd come to the pub after being with family all day—to get away and have time alone.

At that I jumped up, apologizing, to give it to her. She made me sit down again and keep talking.

We shared our stories, sometimes teary, for twenty minutes or more. Then I successfully excused myself to let her leave. My heart eased, I returned to my lukewarm cider, glad I'd followed my hunch. But the experience drained me. I tried to focus on my book. My mind was too fluttery.

I thought she'd left, but she must've detoured to what the Brits call the water closet, because the next thing I knew, she was swerving out of her way to thank me and wish me well. I realized later I'd forgotten her name in my turmoil. I think of her as Helen, which may not be right, but it fits.

This encounter, which I resisted so long, became the saving grace of my trip. I don't know if the prodding I felt came from Tony, her Highlander husband, or the two of them sipping ethereal Scotch and colluding. Maybe she and I were simply vibrating on the same emotional wavelength. Whatever it was, it was weird—how she mesmerized me, how out-of-body I felt, but how certain I was that it was the right thing to do. And the risk paid off richly. Defying common courtesy and my comfort zone turned into a little connection of hearts, a pale echo of the leaps I took in my early days with Tony. The Universe had reminded me why I should trust intuition—probably rolling Its eyes at such a slow learner.

It was still a relief to end that trip and get home, where the energy he'd invested in the walls and ceiling could nurse me. Some days, I could hold my gratitude close and manage activities that would make him proud.

Sometimes just getting through the day is an act of love. Because an incident in a pub was a moment. It dwindled in the legion of moments without him. Everything I do reflects my love for Tony, but everything I do is mourning, too.

Feeding the Dead

The grocery store became unnaturally painful, far more than Tony's funeral. He wasn't there to push the cart, which he'd always commandeered. A handbasket had to do. The shelves taunted me with his favorite foods. More than a year had to pass before the banana display stopped bringing tears to my eyes. His Diet Coke was easier to avoid. I skipped that whole aisle, fighting a sense of obligation to start drinking it for him.

All the cooking I'd joyfully done for us stopped. A complete list of our refrigerator contents, post-Tony:

1. Three cans of dogfood
2. A bag of salad that's out of date but still edible
3. An eight-ounce jar of chicken broth concentrate
4. A half-bag of mini-carrots
5. A gift jar of jelly I may never eat
6. Three Nalgene bottles of chilled water
7. Chocolate

The dog food and the chocolate were the only items sure to be eaten. I would have unplugged this empty vault to save electricity if I didn't need the ice for iced tea.

Food holds symbolic, even spiritual, status. It represents life and love for obvious reasons, but it's equally wound around death.

Not only in funeral casseroles, either. Sugar skulls, heirloom reci-
pes, rosemary for remembrance, and the archetypal symbolism of
Christian communion link feeding ourselves with death to achieve
immortality. I stood in that intersection of food, love, and death that
first Christmas, when I baked my grief into Tony's cookies.

Our only unvarying holiday tradition, these cookies followed a
recipe he had from his dad. We'd made gigantic batches to mail to his
kids. This time, instead of Baking Day Christmas carols, news radio
played in the background. Safer.

Dad Alferio's Italian Cookies

Dough	**Icing**
1 lb. Crisco shortening	1-2 cups powdered sugar
8 cups of flour	3-4 drops almond or vanilla flavoring
1 cup milk	1-2 tablespoons milk
1 cup sugar	
3 tsp baking powder	
1 jar anise seeds	

Measure all ingredients into Tony's prized 18-quart spaghetti sauce
pot. Like he did, squish the whole mess with your hands until dough
forms.

Roll ropes of dough. Fold each rope in half and twist the two
halves together like lovers entwined. Pinch the ends together forever.
Seal with the memory of a kiss. Place on an ungreased or parch-
ment-lined cookie sheet and repeat, twisting love and loss, life and
death, past and present, the old solstice faith with Christmas.

Bake at 350° about 20 minutes or until edges are golden. It won't
be enough time. Cool completely, then sweeten the bitterness of loss
with drizzled-on icing. Sprinkle with tears. (Sugar sprinkles will look
better, though.)

Resist the urge to tip the cookie sheet into the trash. Freeze to maintain sanity and freshness, and eat over time. What choice do we have?

Baking those cookies, like most everything else, brought on an emotional double-vision—seeing Tony beside me in memory and occasionally feeling his spirit even while keenly aware of his absence. Especially in my first four or five months without him, I frequently felt his presence behind me. The weight of his arms wrapped me from behind.

About the time those cookies had all been eaten, I realized it'd been a while since I'd felt his energy. One winter night, just as I'd sadly stopped hoping to feel him, I stepped out to our hot tub. As I flipped back the cover, I froze in the dark. I'd been thinking about nothing but sliding into warm comfort, but the air near the tub was thick with his presence. Involuntarily I said, "Oh! You're here! Thank you." He stayed for a while before the shadows thinned. He had gone.

That might've been the last time he was tangible to me as a full-bodied presence, like he stood in the room. He still came in dreams, and I still sometimes felt an energy like his hands or arms on me. But something subtle in our connection had changed. He'd moved on.

As time passed and the sensation of his presence dulled into memory, I began to question the veracity of those experiences. We all have kinds of awareness we struggle to talk about, let alone understand, including spatial awareness, the feeling that someone is watching, and the proximity of things we can't see. These probably rely on combinations of senses, but they're mostly subconscious—and fallible. The sense of Tony's energy near me was similarly imprecise. My best description is a sort of vibration or buzz that broke into my thoughts or tingled my scalp, ears, and shoulders. As my desire to feel him grew, however, being alert for that sensation became more obvious than the sensation itself. Filled with longing for that sip of love and reassurance, I wondered if I'd been making it up all along. The power of suggestion is real; the power of desire even stronger. Maybe I was only self-soothing.

I can argue both sides of this question. We don't always heed the call of our stomachs, for instance. Those with eating disorders sometimes explain they ignored that voice for so long they have to re-learn how to hear it again. Maybe the voices that resound in our hearts and operate in the shadows of our minds are the same. Dismissing the sense of a dead loved one's presence might be an intuition disorder.

Or am I the one who's disordered? I've gobbled Italian cookies because they tasted good even when my stomach was silent. Do I also binge on the comfort an afterlife offers? A dream visit from Tony, my framed Hershey bars, the hope I will hold him again in some form might be the equivalent of compulsive eating. Nothing will ever shake my conviction that my intuition warned me I would lose him. But how often does my drooling imagination fill in when intuition has nothing to say?

This question became increasingly relevant. The first six months of his absence, I cried every day but was still running on the high-octane fumes of our love and my sense of a Universe that could accommodate fate. By October, the length of forever without him had begun to sink in. My double vision was fading, and his absence, acute, was almost the only thing I could see.

About the time I baked Tony's cookies, the memories that played in the back of my head were competing with growing despair. The deeper the pain, the more I doubted life had any purpose, let alone a spiritual plane or higher consciousness. Darkness accumulated.

The result was not an intuition disorder. The clinical term, I believe, is depression. The only question was whether my intuition, which had led me to Tony and to cherishing him, would starve in the shadow of my misery or strengthen to save me now he was gone.

Meltdown

As depression descended, I fought. In addition to finding a counselor, I binged on self-help. A few of the more exotic ways I tried to cope:

- Quilting a bedspread from Tony's favorite shirts and embroidering it with our favorite sayings so I could sleep under his warmth and humor each night.

- Earning our five minutes of Internet fame as a finalist in a Travelzoo love-story contest.

- Capturing my pain in a grief photography class and random acts of private poetry.

- Inking sorrow into Zendoodles, a calligraphy lesson, and the design for a memorial tattoo.

- Knitting my memories into cowls and a shawl as if fuzzy yarn could replace cuddling.

- Crafting grief into handmade felt, painted rocks, and the bright, broken shards of glass mosaics.

- Dancing with my grief in Soul Motion style, stretching it with grief yoga, and running from it eight miles at a time, sobs sometimes competing for breath.

- Writing it into mantras in Dr. Seuss style—*I will love you here or there. I will love you everywhere*—for sticking on Post-its around the house.

- Sorting sadness with volunteer work organizing donations to a homeless shelter.

- Tackling the "Next Projects" list Tony and I had begun, hammering loss into a remodeled deck and laundry alcove, and feeling Tony's hands in mine on his chop saw and drill.

Almost everything helped. Nothing helped enough.

"I hate to tell you this, but you're a big girl so I know you can handle it," said my dear friend Monica. "Everyone says the second year is worse."

Dutifully I nodded. It couldn't possibly be worse.

Then the seasons passed, slowly, until Tony's Last Day came again. The second year *was* worse. Immeasurably worse. The second year found bloody entrails not already gnawed. Sobs were dredged from deeper in my body. There simply aren't words for the hurt—only gasping, mud, bones.

My experience of grief is that it keeps sinking endlessly in. I can only compare it to my faulty 1970s impressions of a nuclear meltdown: Something deadly burns through its container and then through the floor. It burns through the ground and the dirt and the rock. It keeps sinking, and sinking, and becoming more real, contaminating everything it touches. It glows sickly green, it rips out near China, it punches a permanent hole through the earth.

It contaminated my trust in myself. My heart was too wrenched for me to reside there, so I retreated in large part to my head.

This coping approach was not new for me. Even as Jo Anna's death led me to ideas like reincarnation, it made me seek approval where I could find it. I had to avoid giving my parents more reason to resent me. Maybe if my sister had lived, I'd have still been a straight-A student and "good girl." At minimum, though, my guilt exacerbated those tendencies. Making up for Jo Anna's death was impossible, but I tried to achieve enough for us both, and the thing I was good at was school. Reading, toeing intellectual lines, reciting the answers the system expected—that kept me safe.

Unfortunately, a retreat into reason didn't serve me well this time. The books piled around me on every flat surface ranged from *The Tibetan Book of the Dead* to an atheist's case that spirituality is an evolutionary adaptation, a lie that provided a survival advantage. (You'd think a disconnect from reality would get you eaten by tigers, but in this view, crusades and jihad do more good than harm, effectively outweighing the tigers.) Such intellectual flotsam bobbed with me in a sea of despair. Nothing kept me floating for long.

A Dr. Dubious in me began muttering that half my convictions were bunk. So much of what I know in my heart to be true can be dismissed as coincidence, wishful thinking, or hindsight. Objective confirmation doesn't come often.

In my bouts of embarrassed rationalism, I wasn't alone. A few of my friends and family were too caring to say so, but body language or nervous laughter betrayed how they felt about the "woo-woo" I shared. Their discomfort reflected my own inner conflict. Suspended between reason and intuition, I not only questioned the truth in my heart, I became increasingly distant from who I had been. Tony's girl died by degrees every day.

The more I let rationality overrule my heart, the more toxic my grief became.

I grew desperate.

Sob-Joules and Prickling

If desperation can be measured, its metric in the International System of Units should be a sob, maybe with an energy component: sob-joules. Sob-joules can power a lot of behavior.

The most desperate thing I tried after Tony left was to sign up for a workshop led by David Kessler. Nothing about his therapy itself is extreme, but in addition to his expertise and grief yoga classes led by Paul Denniston, the weekend included sessions with spirit medium Maureen Hancock. By then I'd read several books about mediums or others who claimed to talk with spirits or connect with other planes of existence. One had been written by a journalist with a critical eye. Unconvinced either way, I tried to manage my expectations, aware that attending with the hope of hearing from Tony was a recipe for disappointment. *Focus on David's advice and the yoga.* I gave Tony permission not to make an appearance.

My expectations dropped further when I saw how large the group was—maybe two hundred people. The yoga involved more screaming and pounding than downward dogs, but the workshop's real power lay in witnessing each other's grief. In one session, we took a partner, pressed our hands together, and looked into the other's eyes. Which promptly filled with tears. These were amazing human connections, challenging but validating. The opposite of denial.

My money had been well spent before Maureen took the mic. As she introduced her first session, my hands started tingling with a nearly irresistible impulse to straighten and splay my fingers. During peak experiences I sometimes feel this energy shooting out my fingertips. (*Shazam?*) When it's strong, it spreads so I want to throw my arms wide and my head back to the sky as though I've been cartoon-electrocuted. It's happened miles into an endorphin-fueled run, at the ocean or Grand Canyon, and—TMI warning—frequently when Tony made love with me.

Maureen kept talking through this distracting energy in my hands. Then my scalp started prickling. Sharp! It felt like being poked with a mechanical pencil. That drew my attention up and back to a sense of presence behind me.

A thought entered my head: I didn't need to hear from Tony. I felt him in so many other ways, and plenty of people at the workshop needed more comfort—especially those who'd lost children. Besides, as Maureen described her perceptions of various spirits "pushing through" or "insisting on being heard," I had to smile. Tony wouldn't be pushy or needy in *any* circumstance. If his spirit was there at all, he was either standing back or helping to manage the crowd, convincing others to let the youngest spirits go first.

Only later in the weekend did Maureen say, in effect, "Oh, and when you feel someone behind you but no one's there, and your scalp tingles, that's them! My whole body sometimes tingles, or my hands, blah blah blah. . . ."

Ah, validation.

I left the workshop as uncertain about mediumship as when I arrived. Some of the details Maureen relayed to people were unusual and remarkably specific, difficult to fake. She called out a young woman about a lost fiancé, a pretty good guess simply based on her age. But Maureen continued to talk about a motorcycle accident not long after the loved one proposed. Then she supplied the fiancé's name. The young woman burst into tears as she nodded.

Other cases were less convincing. When Maureen started talking about someone she felt "coming through," ten or twelve participants sometimes raised their hands to identify themselves as a match before Maureen determined whom she felt the message was for. Her descriptions of the departed were woefully broad—"he has a great sense of humor, you spent all your time laughing." Most of the aching audience could relate to such traits, or longed to. The sob-joules in the room were way off the chart, and I contributed my share.

So maybe the witnessing was the best part of the weekend. That's what a hereafter-denier would say. In any instance of denial, however, it's worth asking what value or harm will result. For climate change, the harm seems pretty clear. For messages from the afterlife, not so much. My heart chose to be grateful Tony had a spiritual–mechanical pencil and took the time to poke me with it.

That's admittedly meager proof of a realm beyond this one. But feelings and facts are not the same class of thing. One does not cancel or replace the other. Facts can propel a rocket to the moon, but human emotion is the reason we'd bother, and our hearts' truths are as real as the truths in our heads. Over the course of our lives, the emotions matter more, and living out those feelings and emotional truths may be the only purpose we have. Certainly anyone who cherishes love must agree.

The facts fight for dominance, though. Including the facts that Tony had died, that I woke up and spent most of my days alone, that workshops and sweet dreams were isolated, bright links in a miserable chain. Even when friends had the best of intentions, the path forward from loss was lonely. How could I remain true to my love and my faith when I so rarely felt Tony beside me?

Gradually grief and the length of forever drowned the wisdom in my heart. With my love in danger of being swept away, too, I made some wrong turns and got lost.

Taking Interstate M
South to Failure

During Year 2 AD (Alferio Calendar), I took more trips than I'd like on what my grief counselor and I laughingly called the maladaptive highway. Interstate M runs in the wrong direction. But "highway" implies you might get somewhere you want to go, even if you're shunning the future. It's more like a maladaptive cul-de-sac. I've circled around and around, sometimes escaping down the street for a bit, before finding myself stuck in torment again, my gratitude in the rearview mirror.

Sometimes the cul-de-sac was only slightly unhealthy. I ate more french fries once Tony was gone than in any previous ten years put together. I also transferred some of my grief to my body through miles and miles and hours on foot. So yeah, I started running again. I now understand mortification of the flesh. I ran and cried, ran and remembered, ran until my body forced me to a limp. Physical pain is so much easier to handle. It stays on the surface, not so deep inside. I look like I'm ninety when I rise from a chair, but I'd rather foster arthritis than feel what's in my heart.

In an admittedly more hair-raising lane of Interstate M, I scratched up my skin with an X-Acto blade on nights when nothing else could distract from the pain. Converting grief to stinging blood was surprisingly effective. Besides, something in me wants the loss to leave marks. It's infuriating to look fine on the outside; I need the love and my grief and his absence to *show*. Those scratches weren't big enough. For a while I struggled with the allure of the woodstove and even considered Tony's chop saw or drill. My head knows such urges are crazy, and fortunately, I suppose, I've mostly resisted. But if it can't have Tony, my heart still wants a scar.

Don't talk to me about healing or recovery, both words I reject in the context of grief. There's no healing from this kind of loss, no more than an amputee grows back a leg. There's only endurance and adaptation. The crummy truth is human beings, too resilient by far, get used to having only one leg. Unhappiness defines the much touted "new normal." In place of love, a tall iced tea marked the highlight of my day. When the gulf between love and a cold drink yawned too wide, an X-Acto knife marked my nights.

My maladaptive cul-de-sac would upset Tony enough; it would infuriate him that I usually wish I were dead. I've been traveling too long. I'd like to be done. *Hmm, what's the best way to commit suicide without trauma for whoever found me? If it looked like an accident, would my parents hurt less?* Climbing into the foothills, lying down as if I got lost, and dying of exposure would probably ensure years passed before someone found me. But I'd rather go from our hot tub, where at least I'd be warm. If I tipped my Honda generator into the tub while it was running, would it electrocute me or merely ruin an expensive winter tool?

In conversations, I find myself defending suicide as an answer, which is awkward, since I believe we're not supposed to give up. My past-life regression decades ago included impressions of a young factory worker in early twentieth-century St. Louis—Mary Evans. I don't know the source of what I perceived, but the emotional wallop convinced me it was not my imagination. Abandoned first by her father, who worked on the river, and then through the death of her mother, Mary moved in with a brother she didn't trust who insisted a woman couldn't live on her own. Her bitchy sister-in-law resented her and accused her of stealing the silver. As Mary, I ended an unhappy life with melodramatic defiance, slitting my wrists and bleeding all over that silver. The satisfaction was bitter, the escape a relief. In the darkness that followed, however, my first thought had been, "Oh. I shouldn't have done that." No visions of punishment came. But of course, reincarnation implies any escape is temporary at best.

Still, I've been seriously tempted to leave this life, even knowing I'm lucky in so many ways. The millions of people in far more horrid situations? Unless they simply can't find a weapon, they must know something I don't.

The best rational argument against suicide I've encountered: Good people have to stand shoulder to shoulder against suffering, if not evil, and shirking that duty lets down everyone else. But I don't think I have that much effect on the world. And while I appreciate friends who've told me they'd be crushed, I remain unconvinced my absence would have a lasting effect on anyone but my parents. Any other belief strikes me as egotistical, or at least unrealistic. Relatives and friends in my circle have died. Everyone other than immediate family murmurs, "Gee, that's too bad" and sighs for two weeks before making a donation or similar gesture and going back to their lives as if nothing had happened. The loss joins the other wounds kept in the corner. Those only whimper in moments of quiet.

I'm not suggesting anyone *should* do anything else. Children and dogs and bellies demand to be fed. All who handle these chores despite bloody amputations are discouraged from acknowledging them. Life on this planet only knows how to surge forward. It would continue without me just fine.

Hello, Depression? Is that you? Go away, I'm talking here.

While I don't want to credit my own nihilistic raving, it seems inescapable. Smarter people than me have grappled with this over the last X-thousand years. We know the results. So I don't know why

I keep trying to think my way out. The philosophers concluded that life is not rational but an act of will.

Still, it annoys me that people often condemn suicide without offering a convincing rationale. Particularly those who think there's no life after this! But I'll rain-check my rants about this, because as angry as I am at society's platitudes, I'm more disappointed in myself.

I was once fired by a client who wouldn't say why, and my career as a children's author has gone the way of Old Yeller, but most of my failures have been further from the bone, less of a challenge to who I think I am. The mistakes that led to my divorce, for instance? I'd probably make them again. They reflected my values. Other goofs have been dumb but not character flaws: I once nearly earned a Darwin Award by pouring gasoline on a brush pile that was already burning. (Realizing how stupid that was—three milliseconds after flames rushed up the stream to the gas can—I prevented disaster only by throwing the whole thing onto the fire. *Whoosh!*) But if current events are an indicator, I must've needed more practice with screwing up bigly.

Mission accomplished, I guess. I've never felt like such a failure than in struggling to embrace Tony with more love than pain. Grief often wins. I know he's disappointed. Our relationship shouted about the wonder of love, about recognizing gifts and taking a risk. Now my greasy fingers struggle to hold that wonder. On the worst days, it takes all I've got to defend my unwieldy love against the despair raking claws over it. *I'm trying, sweetheart. It's not good enough, but I'm doing the absolute best I can.*

If there's any excuse for my failure, it's this: "The way you do anything is the way you do everything." Tony embodied that observation himself, and we agreed it was true. He may have hoped for something different, but he knew me and how much we meant to each other. It shouldn't be a surprise that my grief, like our love, has gone to eleven.

For a while, good days would raise hope the worst pain was

behind me. Ha! I no longer expect that to ever be true. I treasure the moments when I feel our love as a mutual thing, when I murmur to him and he seems to answer. I live for the moments when I can blast love to him, surrounding him with sparkles of bright yellow and green, hoping this firehose stream of passion might power whatever he's doing now. But terrible, suicidal days still keep coming.

Dying has never scared me—at least, not since Jo Anna. Without my intense sense of gnosis about our love, all the evidence of fore-knowledge and afterlife signs, it'd be easy to leave. I've had a great life, full of adventure and learning and love, and I still find nature beautiful—and I've had enough.

Three things have kept me from killing myself. Two of them were temporary, and one of those has already passed. I didn't want to leave my geriatric dogs homeless, and I don't want to hurt my parents that much. Tony's dog went to meet him not quite two years later, as I stroked his black fur and whispered, "Go find Tony and tell him I love him." Bape's spirit didn't linger here, so I trust he obeyed. Jazz followed the next year, almost reuniting our pack. My parents are still alive to be wounded, though, and shifting my grief to them would be immoral.

The third reason is selfish and regrettably fear-based. I can't jeopardize my only chance of a Hereafter with Tony. I don't want to flunk soul school. When forced by the sword-point of pain to decide whether life seems more random or purposed, I choose the latter. Because my experiences and emotions suggest patterns and meaning. Frankly, I trust those more than abstract reason.

And if I'm going to make all this noise about premonitions and fate, I must accept an inescapable corollary: Whatever divine plan decreed that Tony's time here was over also dictates I remain here without him, no matter how much I'd like to be done. Gutting it out through every next day seems to be my only path forward. Trying to cheat that destiny is unlikely to earn the Afterlife Bonus Points I may need. I have to keep traveling until I catch up with my sweetheart. I hope my bag's been well-packed by the time I get there.

If I take pride in anything, it's that I keep my commitments, to myself and to others. Like Tony did. I accepted the bargain the Universe gave me. Now I have to live up to it, literally, until the Universe is willing to let me escape. With one eye on the hereafter, I'm doing my best to keep packing my bags: Asking for help, connecting with friends, and seeking the divinity we touched together.

That is the job description of a monk.

PART 5

FOREVER

Monks and Mummies

My second novel takes place in a tenth-century abbey. Monks have long interested me. Their ragged path beckons. As I search for an identity that works for me now, no longer part of a couple and Tony's girl only when I wear his favorite dress, this is the model that seems to fit best. I can wander as a *peregrina*, not in medieval robes but Vasque boots and Gore-Tex. Perhaps my mortification of the flesh from here on out can be limited to blisters and lactic acid.

While exploring this new identity, I stumbled on a five-day workshop sponsored by a group called Abbey of the Arts, which draws connections between artistic energy and divine forces. They offered this "creative spirit" retreat not far from my home, and attending became my way of celebrating Tony's birthday, which occurred the same week. Despite crying a lot, I enjoyed the workshop. In particular, it taught me how dance could help release tough emotions.

Another activity left me more thunderstruck. Initially, I was dubious. Near the end of an emotional and sleep-deprived week, we were asked to make plaster casts of our faces, decorate them, and interact with these identities. Born way before the selfie generation and programmed by my high school culture's disdain for anyone deemed conceited, I resisted this project as narcissistic. Reluctantly I accepted the supplies we would need, expecting this project to be among our least challenging. Hoo-boy, was I wrong.

My partner, Michele, would plaster me first. With a shower cap protecting my hair, I stretched out on a yoga mat and closed my eyes, feeling as vulnerable as a hospital patient. Plastic wrap protected my skin with only the tiniest gap at my nostrils for breathing. Michele began smoothing wet strips of plaster overtop. They were cool, her gentle fingers soothing.

When my eyes and mouth were sealed over, I thought, *Oh! This is like a mummification. I'm being prepared for the next life.* The whole activity was a symbolic death experience, preparing us for a rebirth to the emerging identities we'd try to capture as we painted our dried masks. It fit my grasping after a Joni who had to be here without Tony, preferably one he could be proud of. Or at least one that would temper my wish to be dead. In Tony's terms, she might be Joni 2.0, but I wouldn't consider her any improvement. Backward-compatible at best.

As plaster stiffened over more of my face, the mask felt increasingly isolating. Immobile, I was cut off from the world. I could still feel Michele's fingers and her presence beside me, but I couldn't see or move. I couldn't even breathe deeply. The ethereal music in the room was trance-inducing. Trying to relax, I focused on each shallow breath.

And thought about Tony. This loss of sensation, mobility, control—was it anything like what he had felt as he died? I'd touched his face while I tried to revive him, not in these sweeping strokes but with great urgency. I imagined stroking his stubbled cheeks as Michele smoothed plaster over mine. This could be only the thinnest reflection of dying.

My heart ached so intensely I had to press my hands to my chest. Tears rose. *No. Not now.* Crying was one more thing I couldn't do. If I got sniffy, my slim ability to breathe would be lost and I'd have to bail. But I'm not a quitter. If I were, I would've already drowned myself in the river a half-block from my house.

Michele whispered, "You okay?"

I gave her a thumbs-up. *I can do this. It can't be much longer.* Holding tight to my overwhelmed heart, I tried to anchor myself to the music.

More warm, soothing hands touched my shins, feet, and hands. The workshop leaders had a talent for reading emotion. Sensing my distress, they used gentle contact to tether me to the ground, a balloon—or a ghost—at risk of floating away.

The first teams done with their plastering began to speak above whispers, proof of life beyond my swirling mind and imprisoning mask. I wasn't scared, just awash in emotion: curiosity and grief, loss and uncertainty, gratitude for Michele's tender help. After days spent expressing emotions through movement and sound, those feelings were trapped and roiling. Would my plastering never be done?

Light brightened beyond my eyelids. *Good. Focus on that.* The clouds blocking the sun outside must have drifted. As I appreciated that glow, a sudden impression flashed—*power,* rushing just beyond my eyelids and my sense of self. It was like standing too close to a bison stampede: roaring, immense. The physical sensation, so close, struck me as a divine force, maybe the flow of the collective unconscious. Unlike my vision of spiraling light, which was distant, it was *here,* immanent, both reassuring and intimidating. I almost giggled into my mask because it showed me how utterly inadequate human conceptions of any divinity are. A metaphor jumped to mind, as they always do: We're all ants riding and trying to understand a rocket.

With that, the plastering was finally done. Michele lifted the mask off. *Breathe. Try not to shake.* Light-headed and queasy, I wiped my face and focused on returning the favor for Michele. The softness of her cheeks and the cool glop of the plaster helped calm my trembling fingers. Still, as soon as we'd finished, I had to escape into the woods. To Tony. With the trees and him around me, I could finally cry.

My legs, weighted, would barely move forward. When my tears stopped, still feeling like I'd been hit by a truck, I dropped flat on a patch of pine needles. Arms spread, I stared blindly at the clouds and let my emotions sink into the ground. Surrendering, again. Trying to understand what had happened.

After ten minutes or so, one of the group leaders appeared on the trail. A gift. Though this break in the schedule was her time off to recharge, Betsey kindly paused to sit beside me. She asked and then listened while I spilled my feelings about the mask work, which had veered so far from the lark I'd expected. After brief support and a hug, she walked on. I remained on my back until the chickadees and sparrows hopping through the leaves granted me enough energy to go find warmth and tea.

Though it took me days to recover from that pseudo-mummification, the experience pushed me closer to Tony. Just as I'm learning about grief he already knew, my plastering was a not-very-near-death experience. It gave me one more confirmation of an immensity both in and beyond our perceptions.

Monks and mummies share the assumption of such a Beyond, of transformation to a life after this one. Together, they're leading me forward.

Firefly Magic

Eventually I realized I have a choice, two ways to proceed from Tony's loss. One is the rational way advocated by consumer culture and probably most therapists: Stay busy, swipe right, love again, blah blah blah. That route isn't working for me.

Like a mummy, I choose a less rational way. The word *transformation* may be optimistic, but intense grief does produce someone or something else. A phoenix from the ashes is too grandiose. A firefly feels to me like a better fit. Admittedly, fireflies aren't as attractive, particularly in the daylight and before they can glow, but they aren't phantasms, either. They're a lesser-known symbol of transformation and a liminal link between reality and magic.

Elisabeth Kübler-Ross's position on fireflies, if she had one, does not yield to Google. Her belief in an afterlife, revised over a lifetime as a deathbed doula, isn't referenced as frequently as her five stages of grief—denial, bargaining, anger, depression, and acceptance. This psychology of loss has become a cliché even though she defined the stages for the person dying, not those left behind. Mourners despise them for legitimate reasons, not least because grief resembles a Tilt-a-Whirl more than a set of carved marble steps. Besides, almost any reaction or experience can be distorted enough to be shoved into the model.

Take denial, for instance. Witnessing Tony's death made it hard to deny in any literal sense. Besides, since our romance started out with my bargain, I leaned more on denial while he was alive than after he left. But the oddities I consider signs from him can also be seen as a form of denial, an insistence that he's still here, talking to me. Although few have been as dramatic and hard to explain as the Hershey's Specials, several rank in the same genus as fireflies: quantifiable but still touched with magic.

The Firefly's Grief Personality Quiz

For each example below, identify which are reassuring signs of love and which are denial:

☐ The frog peeping near our bedroom days after Tony left. Frog song is like fireflies for my ears, and we'd often smiled at the croakers in the pond behind our Ohio house. At least a decade had passed since I last heard frogs at my mountain home. Pesticides, climate change, or both had silenced them. When one piped up unexpectedly in those darkest days, I spent twenty minutes hunting the sound, trying to figure out what was making that noise. Phone alert? Low-battery warning? Stereo malfunction? Weird gurgle in a faucet or drain? Eventually I gave in. Only frogs sound like that, and never mind the foot of snow on the ground. Tony was singing to me. Croaks sounded again the next morning as I stepped out of the shower. Frogs are a symbol of transformation; message received. Fireflies would have been even more impressive, but Tony probably had better things to do than defy ecosystems.

☐ The timely luggage cart at the airport just as I asked Tony for help, along with similar answers to questions I've asked in his workshop about the location of tools or how to solve a problem.

☐ The butterfly that lit on my head a few weeks later to halt my crying as I walked in the woods. Frogs and butterflies are natural occurrences, but maybe spirit or consciousness can influence them—or, more likely, me—to draw my attention and soothe me.

☐ The masses of forget-me-nots that appeared in our yard out of nowhere that spring, along with a deluge of robin's eggshells. I spied the first blue shell, three-quarters whole, on the side of a logging road as I jogged. This symbol of Ostara and Easter, and what they stand for, stopped me. Cradled in my palm, it weighed so little that without my eyes I wouldn't have known it was there. Placing it back down gently, I took a few steps and discovered a second a few yards later. This one I picked up and set on a stump so I could retrieve it to take home on my way back. A third lay not far beyond. Siblings from the same nest, perhaps? Two more lay another half-mile along my path. My next hike elsewhere delivered two more, and a couple of weeks later, a third trail brought me three. The total that spring eventually mounted to more than I've found in the entire rest of my life. Many of the shells didn't survive my attempts to keep them, but two halves rest on the kitchen windowsill and another rides in my car. They remind me things that look dead might just be the shell of a less-cramped new life.

☐ The big brown moth, an archetype of messengers, that landed at my fingertips on my laptop keyboard near midnight one snow-blown night. I'd spent an hour or so tearing up over old emails from Tony—including an image he'd used that I had forgotten: "I found myself in Dominica being drawn to yourself, kind of like a moth is drawn to a light. Maybe in your case I should say a firefly being drawn into light. ☺"

"Where did you come from?" I asked my visitor. The size of a credit card, it prevented further typing. No matter. I needed to go to bed, anyhow. Perhaps it had landed to say so, though I preferred to think Tony was letting me know he was still drawn and still with me.

It displayed no interest in fluttering away. "How am I supposed to shut my laptop now?" The moth didn't answer, so I set my computer aside to power down on its own.

The moth was gone in the morning. I expected to find it lifeless on a windowsill or the floor, but I never did. My friend Brenda, when I related this story to her, suggested it lit to remind me to keep seeking light.

☐ The hearts that appear to me everywhere, from sidewalks to skies, echoes of an amber heart necklace Tony bought me. The first appeared while he was still with me in a selfie we almost deleted before I spotted the cause of its overexposure—a remarkable sunburst through the clouds behind our heads. The rays spilling out wreathed us in a glowing heart, turning it into one of my favorite photos.

Another: In a queasy moment after he left, I realized that the watch he gave me for our last Christmas featured hearts, instead of numbers, at the twelve, ten, and five. A heartfelt 4:50—about the time he departed his body. I have to remind myself they're hearts, not some other symbol, for this not to seem creepy.

Less-fraught hearts appeared in a line across his pickup windshield one morning as I embarked on one of my first times camping without him. As best I could tell, rain had dripped off our camper overhang to leave spots, but they were heart-shaped, not round or oblong. Several dozen of the weird watermarks stretched across my field of view like a garland of kisses. They lingered for 150 miles, until wind and bug splatter wore them away. By the time I realized they were fading and tried to take a photo, they had blurred. No one would believe how perfectly heart-shaped they were.

☐ The penny I passed on my bike on a route we'd ridden together. After rolling over its glint, I pedaled for another half mile, feeling nagged, before I stopped, turned around, went back, and found it. Although battered from its life on a forested stretch of Highway 410 where no one should've been sowing pocket change, it's dated 2013, the year I met Tony. I don't buy the superstition that coins are signs from loved ones in heaven. I don't! That's why I kept riding before going back. The odds of a lost penny having any recent mint date are huge. But yeah, I still kept it.

Score yourself: How many of these minor marvels are random? Seven of seven marks a skeptic, while any score lower leaves more room for wonder. But scores of seven and zero are not mutually exclusive. Life is not math. Fireflies in the dark may be insects *and* sparks of joy. I'm dubious, too, of the most common tropes about communication from beyond. Birds lose feathers whether anyone nearby has died lately or not. Nonetheless, I choose to believe in hints of magic instead. That's my interpretation of advice from experts as diverse as Jung, whose definition of synchronicity emphasizes meaning, and Sheryl Sandberg, whose book on grief, *Option B*, recommends we "choose meaning."

I do. It's an exercise in free will. To call it denial denies meaning, too. Even on my worst days, when ceasing to exist sounds more alluring than life, frog croaks and hearts in my path arrest my attention, sometimes when it's distant, to fix it on Tony. If reality permits, they're signs from him. If reality *doesn't* permit, he'd send them if he could. Because he loved me. I know this truth better than I know my own name. The reminder douses me in the feelings we shared, pushing aside at least some of my grief and keeping our love tangible.

Whether you're a skeptic or not, that is what signs are for, and my choice to see them in that light is part of my own metamorphosis, still in progress, from a grub of grief to a spark in the darkness of life.

Bargain Me a Dream

If you're a Kübler-Ross fan, the second stage of grief is bargaining. If you're me, bargaining can be tackled a couple of ways. Within a couple of months of Tony's death, I realized that my version of bargaining was to watch a young couple's wedding or families playing at campgrounds and think sadly, "In our next lives, I want a whole lifetime with you, and maybe kids, too. Okay?" In exchange for such hope, I'd try to survive.

True to a firefly larva, I've moved on to a kind of bargaining that might be even less rational but that lights up dark nights. I trade endurance for the Tony who appears in my dreams.

While I've had a few nightmares, I've had more sweet visions that left my heart singing for hours or days. The first time his birthday arrived without him, he visited my dreams two nights in a row. Dreams of him warmed my heart at his next two birthdays, too. The timing is curious, since I think of him every night, but he visits at other times, too. Frequently we live in separate rooms of a house, where I see him through doorways or out in the yard. It's comforting to feel he's fundamentally close, even if we're stuck on different sides of a wall. These dreams promise someday a door will open and I'll be allowed over a threshold to him.

Better are dreams where I get to embrace him, where our love becomes tactile again. The sensations and emotions are as real and as rich as they used to be when I was awake. Our brains, research shows, do not know the difference. Sweet dreams like this defy death and time, bringing us together imaginatively. Life's painful again when these liaisons fade, but they're still a gift of his love and our continued connection.

Sometimes he's just there, accompanying me while I go about my subconscious business. We've been shopping in dreamland, attending a conference, and squeezing under a bed together to find time alone in a crowded hotel room. His appearances in these dreams, so mundane, don't rival the emotional impact of more gripping visitations, but their casual closeness is tenderly sweet. They make our bond feel habitual still.

By far the best dream came near Tony's second birthday away. In a grove with a *Midsummer Night's Dream* atmosphere, sparkles filled the trees like fireflies. I wore a silky white dress that made me feel young. Flowers in hand, I was rehearsing for my wedding to Tony. My mother and uncle had arrived early to watch. Though I struggled to remember the words of our vows in the right order, I wasn't worried about getting it wrong. I was too overjoyed.

When the time came, though, the magic leaked out of the grove. The sparkles and family members were gone. After positioning myself on the grassy knoll for the ceremony, I realized I'd been mistaken. No wonder the vows had been elusive; it wasn't my wedding. I'd been rehearsing as a stand-in—or interloper.

I know where this feeling comes from. The interval between Lynetta's death and Tony's was brief. Despite the horror of her situation, I can't help but feel sometimes like she won.

I know in my heart that he loved me. I'm pretty sure that if he'd had a choice, he'd have stayed here with me for longer than he did. But that doesn't stop me from sobbing on bad days, when despair whispers that he left me to go back to her.

Is she a more-evolved soul who deserves his time more? Probably. Alzheimer's seems like a trial to burnish the saintly. We can only hope such suffering has purpose in it.

Fortunately, that disappointment wasn't the end of my dream. My flowers drooping, my heart crushed, I crumpled to a seat on a rock. Tony wouldn't be coming. If he did, he wasn't coming for me. But then there he was striding toward me, taking my free hand to pull me to my feet. As he led me across the clearing toward a creek, I understood we were already united. We didn't need the ceremony I'd been rehearsing. We didn't need the audience or flowers or vows. We only had to cross that water together, and even in my dream I realized the creek was a symbol for the boundary between life and death.

The dream bled into waking, where I basked in it. No, we hadn't had a literal marriage, but our spiritual union endured. When the rehearsals and performance of this life were over, I could look forward to being with him. Until then, he'd be waiting on the other side of that creek.

Maybe Freud was right and such dreams are wishful thinking—my subconscious struggling desperately to negotiate life and still have Tony, too. The comfort of these dreams is still valid.

Freud was a sex-obsessed nut, though. If you ask me, Jung got more correct. His attention to dreams shaped his life and success, and he had a near-death experience, too. He's fallen out of favor among the shrink glitterati for various reasons, including a rationalist bias that dismisses anything it can't test rather than doing what we can to explore it. Today more therapists promote reasoning our way to mental health with cognitive behavioral therapy. That kind of therapy has helped me, but my encounters with the unconscious, mine and the collective's, help more. They touch far more emotion and offer more meaning.

Full disclosure, however: I've had a few nightmares, too, in which Tony's alive but doesn't want to be with me. In these, I've made some mistake he will not forgive, refusing me any chance to apologize or explain. Such nightmares are murky, like the emotions in them, and I'm grateful they're brief and undetailed. I wake myself crying as it is.

The only value I can find in nightmares like this are the spotlight they shine on my most secret fears.

When I mentioned these nightmares to a friend who does dream-work, she led me to a revelation: The blame I felt for Jo Anna's death became a buried conviction that if somebody leaves me, it must be my fault. Her suggestion hit me with a scalp-prickling rush, my body confirming what my conscious mind couldn't see. The nightmares have not recurred since. Score one for dream therapy! If they do return, I'll use them as a prompt to reread old emails, study Tony's grin in our photos, and embrace beloved memories. Abundant evidence helps me recall the truth of our love and cement it again in my heart.

Between the sweet visitations and nightmares is a theatre stage. Since Tony left I've had a recurrent dream that doesn't involve Tony but still reassures me. These dreams land me in theatrical productions that go awry because I didn't realize I was acting and haven't seen a script. "All the world's a stage, and all the men and women merely players," quoth the Bard, implying a predestined story, if not a director or audience. While bewildered to find myself on a stage and incapable of giving my fellow actors the cues they expect, I always manage to improvise.

One interpretation, of course, is that I am scrambling to figure out what to do or say next, to respond in some way that's expected of me. The muddle is real, no doubt about that, though I don't think I care what's expected. More important, these dreams resonate happily for me because I always wake with the understanding that life is both fiction and temporary. Nothing happening here matters, and ad lib is okay. I just can't spoil the play by shrieking and running offstage. The show must go on but will eventually end. Suicidal impulse, take note.

In the meantime, I close my eyes every night on the hope that my sweetheart might appear. My chances to hug him in dreams don't come often enough, but I cherish each. He never says a word, but the new bargain I've made is to believe that once I finally join him offstage, he will.

Break Glass in Case
of Emergency

Anger, the third stage of loss, has troubled me less than it does some bereaved souls, probably because the Universe gave me so much warning. After that favor, resentment seems churlish. Still, from my first morning alone, I could not bear to see myself in a mirror. I still can't. The contrast with the glowing me who stood there moments before is too stark. My reflection shouts proof that it's not a bad dream. More than an instant of that new, hated me fills me with an urge to throw something and break her. I learned to dry my hair and apply eyeliner by feel.

Protecting my bathroom mirror spurred an alternate impulse to throw rocks through windows, my own or the neighbors'. This itch was more than a will to destroy. I longed to break the glass between present and past, the barrier between this world and the next. Having glimpsed the other side of that one-way mirror, I suspect the scrim, if I could aim correctly to hit it, is fragile.

Practical, I tried to channel the urge to break things. After a number of failures—success. Of a sort.

US Trademark Application

Filing Date: May 2018

Industry: Self-help

Nature of the product: Anger management

Product concept: An alternative to neighborhood vandalism

Market: The bereaved

Product prototype 1: Stomped kindling. (Disadvantage: Trademark applicant is required to stomp kindling all winter anyway; intended benefits could not be realized.)

Product prototype 2: Bottles swiped from recycling bins and smashed on boulders. (Disadvantages: Potential theft charges, hazardous waste.)

Competing service: A Seattle business called Let's Bust Shit Up, where customers can pay to swing hammers at computers and glass. (Disadvantage: A two-hour drive away.)

Use instructions: Buy eighteen eggs. Eat three over several breakfasts. Using a Sharpie, write a detail or aspect of your grievance on the shell of each of the remaining eggs. (Example: The top fifteen things I hated about losing Tony.) One by one, announce each grievance aloud and hurl its egg against a tree stump. *Caution*: Egg goo and tears may splatter. Use at your own risk. Safety glasses recommended.

Cleanup: Dogs may safely lick up product remnants.

Desired trademark: Throwing Eggs™

Slogan 1: Unleash Your Inner Vandal℠

Unique selling proposition: Don't Break Down—Break
  Throwing Eggs™!

Product advantages: Cheap, cathartic.

Throwing Eggs™ earned the approval of my therapist and probably warrant a pitch on Shark Tank. Their practicality puzzles me, though. Why is it socially acceptable to hear our hearts rage and to unleash that anger in action, while more benign murmurs may be dismissed as illusion and attempts to express them squashed or ridiculed? Is anger more scientific, easier to plot on a scale? Or simply more suited to patriarchy? Feminist scholars have noted that feelings and experience have "traditionally been seen as a source of women's knowledge."[2] Rationality, the domain of men until quite recently, was therefore prioritized, along with the aggression often driven by anger.

More Throwing Eggs™ have been hurled since my first proof-of-concept, but their satisfaction wanes once the carton is empty. Bargaining and denial provide more lasting solace. Dream visitations and signs grow more rare for me as time passes, but my heart still stutters at each, freshening my love more than skepticism can. That's a reaction I see no reason to correct.

Not Acceptance but Action

D epression, the only Kübler-Ross stage of grief I can't argue with, has already sucked up enough oxygen. The final stage is acceptance. Say good-bye to Elisabeth Kubler-Ross, though, because here's where she and I part ways forever.

Acceptance is a form of surrender, a word whose meaning I've only recently grasped. For a couple of years now, I've tried to surrender—to love, to the Divine, to my fate. But the tranquility I could glimpse in the early days has receded, and the calm of capitulation wears off. Pain oozes through. I get mad and resist. I cry and despair. I've had to surrender again and again, and the white flag hasn't led me anywhere good. It's too passive. Surrender is helpless, hopeless, resigned—a Three Stooges trio jointly known as depression, and not conducive to feeling my love.

So I'm not going to surrender. I'm skipping "acceptance." Other A-words fit better. Adjustment, for instance. Adjustment describes the process more accurately while giving me more agency.

Not that adjustment is easy. After more than two years of desperate grieving, life still felt intolerable, leaving me with a choice: Kill myself, my parents be damned, or find some new perspective. I'd tried every grief recommendation known to humanity, and if I kept doing the same things, I was going to keep feeling the same way.

One day in the spring of 2019 I was out for a run, appreciating the forested foothills and thinking about this recognition literally. Something had to change. What?

All I could control was my own perspective. Recalling how in my first months with Tony I wondered if I'd overlooked my own death and gone to heaven, I thought, *What if* I'm *the one who died and* this *is the afterlife?*

It's no fantasy. This is certainly my after-Tony-life.

Welcome to Sunny Paradise!
Courtesy of the Afterlife Chamber of Commerce

Put down your suitcases! We're so glad you're here at this legendary travel destination. Let's start by debunking some misconceptions.

True or false?

The Afterlife, aka heaven, is a flower-strewn meadow.
False. Not *this* afterlife, anyhow. In fact, you may find this afterlife disappointingly similar to Earth. But it's huge—especially compared to one lousy meadow. There's so much to explore.

The Afterlife is pleasant and everyone is happy.
False. There's pain and confusion and ugliness here, and enlightenment is not on display. Sorry.

Wait. This afterlife must actually be Hell.
False. Look around. It's far too beautiful for that. And get a load of our most famous attractions!

Popular Afterlife Attractions

The Life Review

You've got loads of great memories. Free admission, but may evoke tears.

The Paradise Periscope

Look back on loved ones left behind, make sure they're okay, and watch over them.

Our apologies, but the Periscope is closed indefinitely. You'll just have to trust that anyone you've been parted from is well and still loves you.

Reunions with Your Beloved

This attraction operates on an irregular schedule and with short notice. But be patient—you might get lucky!

Afterlife FAQs

Q: You mean I'm here for eternity?
A: Or until further notice. It'll feel the same.

Q: Shouldn't I be playing a harp?
A: Who gave you that idea?

Q: Isn't there some One here on a throne I'm supposed to be worshipping?
A: None who's so insecure as to demand worship from the likes of you.

Q: Do I need to pass any test or earn wings?

A: No. You're in the Afterlife. Goals and plans are back in the land of the living. Either you achieved enough to get here, or achievements don't matter. Our best information suggests it's the latter.

Things to Do in This Afterlife

Once you've checked out this Afterlife's most famous attractions, you may be wondering how to make the most of your valuable time. The concierge doesn't recommend depression. We do hope you'll be kind to other guests you may meet. Otherwise, being here is all that's expected.

Later that week, I had a session with my grief counselor, Danielle. A gentle blonde with something of the Southern belle about her, she began, as usual, by balancing her laptop on her knees and asking brightly, "Well, what's going on, Miss Joni?"

Curled into the corner of the couch opposite her, I told her about the new perspective I'd been musing.

She laughed. "Oh my goodness, mama!" She's fond of this term of endearment, though she's well aware I don't have kids. Otherwise, her exact words haven't stuck in my memory the way many of my conversations with Tony had, but she added something to the effect of, "Leave it to you—you're one of my 'thinkers.' That is different, all right!"

I explained, "Thinking about my life this way, as though he's the one who's still alive, makes it easier for me to wait for him to get here."

"I'm in favor of things that make it easier." She smiled. "As long as they're not what you enjoy calling the 'maladaptive highway.'"

The leather of her couch beneath me was cold. A fuzzy throw lay alongside me, but her office makes me mindful of body language, so I didn't pull it into my lap. I'd noticed I tended to self-soothe with it, which appealed as I got to the sticking point in my afterlife analogy. "But how do I fill the time? There doesn't appear to be anything I'm supposed to do, and I don't feel like I have any purpose. I'm just taking up space." It didn't help that the kids' books I'd been steadily working on were being met variously with crickets or a resounding chorus of "meh."

"I'm quite convinced you do have a purpose," said Danielle.

We'd discussed this point before. Unfortunately, her conviction wasn't contagious. Instead of repeating my doubt, I replied, "I keep thinking about what Tony would want me to do if I were in the afterlife and he wasn't."

"It sounds like you knew him well enough to know."

I nodded. "That's easy." He'd tell me to dive into Heavenly seas. He'd push me to explore this world's less familiar locations, to take our little camper on Afterlife road trips like, but unlike, those we'd dreamed of taking, jaunts to Cloud Nine Colorado and Hereafter New England.

Traveling without him had been so miserable, though!

Divine insight: If I'm going to be miserable either way, I might as well make Tony proud. Since there's no Paradise Periscope I can use to spy on him, all I can do is send love back to him and hope he can feel it. I can't know. It has to be enough that *I* feel it. Meanwhile, I have to better embody who we were together and what our relationship stood for—adventures, playfulness, loyalty, second chances. At least then I could feel like less of a failure and more like I might be earning time with him later.

"I think that's a wonderful perspective," said Danielle as I explained this insight to her—and myself.

My therapist may give me too much praise and too little tough love, but this perspective reversal has proven useful. Actions are the key to this after-Tony-life. Another A-word in his honor.

"Happiness is an act of will." We've all heard it, but I've mostly ignored it. The bulk of my life has been organically happy. When it wasn't, the homily didn't make sense. The longer I study Emotions 101, the less I believe we can control our feelings, and losing Tony has only reinforced that opinion. Maybe grad students can be happy or sad by force of will, but I'm just a sophomore. I can't.

"Life is an act of will." "Love is an act of will." "Faith is an act of will." People are attached to this phrasing. It's dawned on me that in every case, the operative word isn't *will*. It's *act*.

Do something. The phrase "fake it till you make it" has never appealed to me. It promotes dishonesty and inauthenticity, both of which contradict true achievement. Case in point: My less-suicidal days contrast with the bad ones mostly because they're more numb. Going through life by rote—the acclaimed staying busy—I feel *less*, not better. Nope, I'm not settling for that. My objective is to feel our love, to hold Tony closer inside me than the grief. Faking that I'm okay with his absence is not a solution.

But aiming to feel different by doing something I'm not sure I want to do is another way to interpret "faking it until you make it." A trip to Afterlife Hawaii without him might hurt terribly, but it's unlikely to be numb. At minimum I'd feel more like I'm being true to us both—the opposite of faking. And love is a verb.

This became tangible in my hunt for our septic tank.

Digging Deep

Determined to be a trooper and act, I pulled on Tony's oversized leather work gloves. I have my own that fit better. I prefer slipping on his. This way I can still hold his hand.

The old shovel is mine. The septic tank—the alternative for rural homes not served by a sewer—is all mine again, too, along with the knowledge that it ought to be pumped out. (The recommendations vary, and my use was a fraction of the system's designed capacity, but it hadn't been pumped since I bought the house. It was long overdue.)

After digging a while, I handed the shovel to the pumper-truck's driver, who was kind enough not to laugh at my efforts but couldn't afford to be here all day.

His superior skill didn't matter. The septic tank was not where it was supposed to be. Not per the previous owner's description and not per the county's as-built diagram. The missing tank mocked my longing for Tony. He would have handled this dilemma—or at least we'd have faced it together.

Nearly an hour of searching and pipe-tracing later, the expert's conclusion was stark: "The tank is under the building." He leaned the shovel against the offending wall, one side of the workshop that matches the house. "Call me back when I can get to the lid."

My home's original owner had built his shed over the septic tank. Why? But I was responsible, too. When Tony decided to convert part of our enormous woodshed into a workshop, I'd trusted the as-built, which located the tank between the buildings. Not in one. Tony added a wall, moved cords of wood—and installed joists and flooring in the section he'd claimed. The work enabled his fancier kitchen remodel, and his conversion of "my" home into "ours" pleased us both.

Now I had to undo his work. As if his absence wasn't enough.

My brother once worked in the septic industry. I texted him, trying to practice my new skill of leaning on others.

Or not. He joked about renting me a bulldozer but didn't offer to help.

Once more pulling on Tony's gloves, I dropped to my knees and began prying up the OSB panels he'd put down for his workshop floor. The tortured nails squealed.

I'm sorry, sweetheart. My tears dripped into the dust. *I hate this even more than you would.*

Tony believed in doing things right, but far more nails were installed than squeak-free flooring requires. Those brass nails shared a secret: Some big kid enjoyed the nail gun he'd bought for this project. I heard its echoes: *Bam! Bam!* Where he hammered, I pried. My kneecaps grew sore but my grief lifted a bit. *You had fun with that new toy, huh?*

I was forced to cut panels that vanished, like the septic pipe, under a wall. Taking a deep breath, I gripped Tony's circular saw. It's heavy, not made for my much-smaller hands. *Help me steady this thing and cut halfway straight, will you?*

The saw smoked and whined about my technique, but the sense of Tony's arms around mine kept it cutting—more wavy than straight, but without the kickback I dreaded.

Eventually my shovel clanked on the tank, a hollow sound like a graverobber striking a coffin. No theft this time. I felt more like something stolen had been returned, broken but still recognizable. Welcome. I'd heard Tony's voice, felt his arms, been inhabited by him.

Once the tank was pumped, I spent another full day replacing his floor. I enjoyed that time with his ghost even more, kneeling in the same spots and building what he built instead of undoing his work. His noisy nail gun was gone, claimed by his son, who'd driven from Kentucky five months after Tony had died to take his boat, many tools, and a few items of furniture his kids had rightly inherited. It'd been hard to watch as the yellow boat trundled away, simply because we'd enjoyed it so much together, but his family, and his son, had used it even more. I knew Tony wanted him to have it. For solace I kept Tony's favorite small tool, a drill-driver of nearly the same bright yellow. As I replaced his flooring, it drove long screws to fasten him more firmly to me.

At last I understood the advice to "stay busy"—or unearthed an interpretation that works better for me. Grief has too much in common with a septic tank. Few people want to acknowledge it, let alone get hands-on. But hands-on action is my only way to stumble forward. The deck addition we planned, the new closet doors, the coffee table Tony promised to make: These new projects we expected to tackle together offer my surest chance to still feel his love, embodied in his handiwork, his tools, and his gloves.

Comfort can be buried in unexpected places. Tony wouldn't have wished a lost septic tank on me, but taking responsibility—action— was an ethos we shared. "Doing what your loved one would want" is not a novel concept, even for me. The journal I started four days after he left offers proof. Its pages are full of missing words and illegible scrawls. Yet there's wisdom there, too. The shaky lines show how in some ways, I've come a circle. (Score one for the Tilt-A-Whirl model of grief, which I hereby upgrade to a Slinky—an unstable spiral, dizzying rounds but with a strip you can follow forward.) Over and over in that journal I wrote, "Our love is strong enough to transcend death." I kept telling myself to hang onto the joy, the ways he changed me, the wonder and possibility he revealed in the Universe for me.

That last one—possibility—matters as much as action. The two relate intimately, exactly as they did when we took risky actions to pursue the possibility of love. The parallel should have become clear to me sooner, but embracing the potential for the miraculous and acting on it are interdependent. A septic tank cleanout is fine, but only the notion that Tony could help me elevated it to an echo of love. Until now, some of the actions I've taken haven't supported me as well as they could because when I'm rational—it does happen— the prospect of X years without him, Y flights with no Tony in the plane seat beside me, and Z years in this pain lead straight to despair. Despair blares louder than action alone.

Another ingredient is needed for possibility to erupt, and I think at last I've found it. For this firefly glowworm, life is not an act of will. It's an act of imagination.

Imagination transforms. It's worked for me before. While in college, I strayed from the wonder of science only when the mathematical answers of physics grew boring. Literature classes acknowledged human feelings, and any answer I could support was correct.

That move in college from science to arts chucked aside reason for imagination. Looking back, that's a choice I've made more than once.

Once more, enter Jo Anna, stage left.

Acts of Imagination

Despite my teen efforts to contact my dead sister by séance or Ouija board, she only visited once, decades later. One gloomy night following my divorce, I lay in bed feeling sorry for myself, sobbing through Episode 1 of *How to Escape This Planet Without Killing Your Parents*. My dogs snored downstairs, the house otherwise silent. Streetlight filtered through the trees and in through the window near the foot of my bed.

A large dark figure strode through the doorway and alongside the bed.

Invader! I sat bolt upright. Fragments of profanity and questions flew through my mind—*How upstairs? So quiet! The hell, dogs? Shit! Martial arts—ready?*

The dark shape never paused, flowing out through the window to mix with the shadows. No one was there. A girl's giggle chimed like glass through my mind, echoing.

I knew at once it was Jo Anna and why she had come—to startle me out of self-pity and remind me of a more comprehensive perspective. It worked. She was right. I snapped on the light and sat stunned, still hearing her naughty delight at spooking me, while absorbing the message that my problems deserved more laughter than tears.

Nothing about that seemed rational, and it may have been no more than imagination. Yet it proved too useful to dismiss. That evening would not be my last descent into self-pity, obviously, but it marked a turning point in my adjustment to divorce. It also helped prompt my first adult introspection about Jo Anna's death and the ways she has shaped me without being here.

For a while I played with automatic writing, hoping to hear more from her. I started with the relaxation of self-hypnosis. My pen left line after line of loops on my paper as I thought of the day of her death, as well as that night in my bedroom, and asked her to take over the pen to speak. I listened for out-of-place thoughts that might be her voice in my mind. Now and then I wrote one down.

Other times I began by writing to her, musing over what I recalled of that day, following my stream-of-consciousness, apologizing. She'd never learned to read, of course, let alone write, but if a spirit could take control of my pen, literacy seemed like a small obstacle. Besides, the laughter I'd heard during her recent visit had been girlish but not a toddler's.

Later I scanned the lines for any words that jumped out. Had she left me a message? The ink on the page never felt supernatural, but it served as invaluable therapy as well as prompting a novel I haven't published but consider my best. Throwing myself into drafts of that novel and others helped heal the wounds of divorce.

My guilt about her still took a long time to wane. The final trick had been meeting Tony's grandnieces in Ohio. Two bright little girls, they made me think of Jo Anna. They nearly matched her age and mine when she died. Watching them play I realized, finally, that no child so young was responsible for *anything* that happened. Making mistakes is their job—it's called learning—and parents can't control everything. Jo Anna's death was a tragedy, but not one with someone to blame.

My friend Monica has suggested that perhaps my bargain for Tony was actually another tip from my sister, warning me to love him full force while I could. What resonates more intensely for me is that Something in or around us hums of everything we need to know, if we'll open our hearts to listen. Jo Anna's death merely taught me to pay attention to possibilities that aren't on the surface. Her appearance years later, even if only through the medium of my imagination, pushed me into actions that benefited me.

Imagination and intuition are not the same thing, but flexing one seems to awaken the other. Perhaps that harmonic resonance has attuned my heart, too, because my fiction has displayed an ominous tendency toward foresight.

For years I worked on a novel manuscript involving an unusual love triangle. When I couldn't make it work, I abandoned the story—not long before an unusual love triangle upended my marriage. That left *me* abandoned. A rationalist might say my subconscious recreated an issue I was interested in, although that denies the agency of the other people involved. Not to mention requiring a masochistic subconscious. To me the sequence speaks more of a lesson for my soul and a creative instinct to explore the same themes.

Which is why I've been musing a scene in another of my novels written more than ten years ago. Writing has always helped me understand life, and this scene apparently came to me early. Near the end of the book, the heroine, Ariel, and her father figure, Scarl, talk about grief:

"It hurts terribly, doesn't it? Losing people you love. Even for a short while."

"It's not always a short while," [Ariel] said flatly. "It's sometimes forever."

He rose and resettled awkwardly beside her to cradle her shoulders. "So it seems."

"How can you stand it?" she asked, not thinking of anyone in particular, just desperately needing the adult in her life to have an answer.

He rested his chin on her head. "You can't," he whispered into her hair. "You can't stand it, Ariel. You pretend, that's all."

"But why?"

"Because others are pretending, too, I suppose. You do it for them."

As she opened her mouth to question, he unsnarled a twig from her hair. The gesture made his point better than all argument.

"You pretend for me and I'll pretend for you?" she murmured.

"Exactly." He smiled unconvincingly. "And when one of us leaves the world, the other will find someone else to pretend for. That's what people do. Because the world is pretend, Ariel, all of it. It's one long and layered, make-believe tale—just a bead on a very big abacus."

Ariel pondered his words. So much pretending seemed like a lot of trouble, and inside out, somehow. She could feel, too, that he was trying to skip over his own loneliness and doubt. That was what he meant, she supposed, by pretending, and the fact that he needed to do it hurt her, but it also showed that he loved her and was trying to comfort her. She sighed and rested her head on his shoulder, unaware of how much her motion comforted him.

He touched the [abacus] beads at her throat. "You have many stories to live yet, and plenty of people to love. Even if they aren't here in your necklace today."

Her fingertips rose to her abacus, too . . . If the world was only a story, as Scarl claimed—and she suspected his words contained truth—it was filled with genuine magic as well as pretending.

Though I'd had painful losses by the time these words were published, those hurts were nothing like losing Tony. I would wonder what in my experience had even prompted this scene except all three books in that trilogy came to me from Beyond as if I were transcribing a voice. On bad days the hope in this scene doesn't convince me, but I'm quite sure it should. That's why the words were dictated to me.

Pretending is an act of imagination, one that transforms the pretender and her audience. Like Ariel, I despise pretending that I'm bearing my loss, that I'm even within shouting distance of okay. Honesty informed my relationship with Tony, and losing him has decimated my already meager patience for bullshit. If there's anyone I can pretend for, however, it's him.

Plus the difference between faking and pretending matters. While fakery is a rational way to deceive someone else, pretending suspends reason to usher in magic.

In a theatre, this is called "acting." Imagination is what gives the actions meaning. Without it, actions are merely chores—"staying busy."

Am I playing word games to endure the intolerable? My answer and endurance change from one day to the next. But humans have always relied on stories to make their lives tolerable, whether in the form of legends, paperback novels, or Netflix. Add spiritual beliefs to the list if you like. I still choose imagination and the meaning it creates.

My ambivalence about pretending aside, my heroine was correct that the world offers genuine magic to console us. I only need to picture one face to be sure. As I pretend to get through each day, my most important action is to point out for myself, again and again, the magic we shared.

In the end, Tony is my best proof of a numinous world and an afterlife that may be part of it. Whether the Universe plays *Let's Make a Deal* in any factual sense doesn't matter. I know heaven exists because I lived there with him. That he appeared in my life, loved me, and would chance a new start with me—it felt then and still feels miraculous. I think we both knew we didn't have much time. That hunch helped deepen our love and glorify our adventures. Our fairy-tale romance suggests an unseen design, a blind embossing that can't be explained but was felt by our hearts and followed. Not unlike the dictation of my most successful book.

Writing has long been my way to answer the questions I can't figure out. Apparently even when I find—or am handed—an answer, I have to convince myself again and again: Act. Imaginatively. Even irrationally.

In other words, keep following intuition. I recently followed mine to a vision fast in a desert. It rewarded me with slivers of joy—and, yes, a vision.

Rituals with Rocks

D eath Valley. It's one of my favorite places, a national park Tony and I enjoyed together and one I had visited at least twice before. In my late-night supplication of Google for oddball new ways to act with imagination, I came across an organization that runs vision fasts in the Valley. I wasted no time signing up.

The vision quest tradition has long interested me for the same reason scuba diving and backpacking do—I appreciate nature, a physical challenge, and the chance for unusual sights. To take that challenge in a landscape I adore, four years to the day since Tony and I went there together, sounded too good to be true. Aware I needed a rite of transition, a swift kick into whatever my life should be now, I hoped to find some inner direction.

By the time the dates rolled around, though, I considered forfeiting the money I'd paid and not going. My heart knew that high on the fortnight's agenda would be saying good-bye to Tony. One way or another. You can't perform a rite of passage to find a new start without also marking an ending.

But I also knew I had to do it. Bitter medicine might be best swallowed under blue sky in a timeless place I find sacred. Even its name seemed to fit my objectives.

The people who assembled on our first day together were an eclectic bunch whose only common interest seemed to be nature. Ranging in age from seventy-three to twenty-three, they included a New York

attorney, a painting contractor, an anthropology professor, a therapist, a professional musician, a social justice warrior Buddhist, a
barista, two gig-working nomads, and a genuine mountain man who
distills essential oils. Our guides surprised me even more. A mid-
dle-aged cowboy sent by Central Casting deferred to a hippie-artist
who must have been pushing seventy but who fused Barbara Walters
with Strega Nona.

Led by this pair of wilderness therapists, our group bounced over
the rutted road to our remote campsite, bonding fast. The first few
days were devoted to introspection, group support, and practical matters. As the guides grilled us on why we'd come and what we hoped
to achieve, even the men all shed tears. The wisdom and insights of
both guides were remarkable even before the big challenge at the
heart of the course. The desert heat I'd expected didn't materialize.
Ice froze my water bottle and howled in the wind, but the warmth of
the group—supplemented by a spare down blanket and every stitch
of clothing I'd brought, all worn at once—made it tolerable. To bless
the adventure, a desert fox walked past me, an arm's length from my
open tent, on my first evening as I was preparing for bed. I couldn't
have asked this Trickster messenger for a more auspicious start.

Every participant chose a different focus for the four days and
nights we would spend alone and hungry. Claiming adult indepen-
dence, marking a fortieth birthday, and embracing elder status were
recurrent themes. Our preparation emphasized creating rituals with
the materials around us to focus our emotions, insights, ideas, and
plans. When we scattered to find campsites out of sight of each other,
I arranged my sleeping bag in a hollow near a pygmy cedar bush
surrounded by protective boulders. In addition to some shelter from
the wind, this spot lay adjacent to a narrow, flat ridge with a clear
view of sunset, mountains, and moonrise. When I saw it, I knew I'd
lay my beloved to rest there.

The four days of my fast passed in leisurely conversations with a local lizard, long walks through the stony desert, the voice of a makeshift drum heralding the rise of the full moon, glittering stars, and lumpy sleep on rocks after my inflatable sleeping pad died. My most important ritual, which I began the second day, was building a rock cairn for Tony.

I collected a few dozen sizeable stones that appealed to me, one for each of his best qualities, from his deep voice to his generosity and humor. White quartz, black basalt, sandstone of orange, yellow, and red. Their textures chapped my fingertips. Distinctive stones fill this particular part of the Valley, so it wasn't hard to recall what each one stood for. My favorite was an obvious heart shape of dark gray fringed with white mineral crystals. Cantaloupe-sized, it became Tony's big heart.

In desert silence so deep it was almost a roar, I placed each rock while naming aloud the trait it stood for. Once it felt complete, I circled my cairn, weeping and talking to and appreciating him. Circling and circling hypnotized me. With blue sky as my witness and the breeze sighing past, memories rose as examples for certain rocks and their traits.

Eventually a voice in my head said, "It is done." I whispered goodbye before turning my back on the cairn and retreating down the slope to my camp.

Once the moon rose, I hauled my sleeping bag up and slept by the cairn as though at his side. Roaring wind woke me midway through the night. It snatched off my down blanket, which I had to hunt down, but it also seemed to honor the storm of my grief. I lay awake in its furor, staring at the cloud-filled black sky. People talk about grief coming in waves, but the wind makes a better metaphor than a rhythmic sea—sweet memories floating on a gentle breeze one moment, unpredictable gusts and scouring destruction another.

My last afternoon alone, I climbed again to the cairn. This time I removed each rock I'd placed. Expressing gratitude for the trait it represented, I turned and flung it as far as I could, tossing Tony's gifts back to the wind and the earth. This symbolic equivalent of scattering ashes spent more furious energy than my throwing eggs had. The weight of the rocks yanked my hand, arm, and ribcage. Each struck the stony ground with the crack of a rifle. The echoes ricocheted through my heart.

Only one stone remained—the gray-and-white heart-stone. I brought that one down with me. I intended to leave it where I'd slept when I left. Before I even sat down, inspiration hit me.

Earlier in the week I'd hiked toward the tail of our gulch to an ancient pictograph rock our guides had mentioned. While there I'd noticed several sentinel stones overlooking it from the hillside nearby. From below, it was impossible to tell if these tall, slender stones jutted naturally from the bedrock or perhaps had been placed by the Timbisha–Shoshone people who still live in the park.

I'd decided to find out. The only likely route for climbing up the steep scree started at a hollow at one side of the hill. The slope above wasn't so sharp. As I approached, I'd been daunted by two enormous boulders with lava eruptions like warts that sat on either side of the hollow, one slightly ahead of the other. These threshold guardians couldn't have been more forbidding with "Do Not Enter, Joni" spray-painted on them. That energy turned me away. With a last glance at the sentinels, I'd returned to our camp.

Now, once I'd scattered the cairn marking my love, I became abruptly aware I had one more ritual task. The perfect place to leave the last one, Tony's heart-stone, would be under the watchful gaze of those sentinel stones, preferably right at their feet. If the guardian boulders would let me. If I could climb the slope beyond them after not eating for four days. And if the sentinel stones seemed amenable to me leaving that charge.

By the time this notion struck me, the sun was already low. Not sure I could hike that far and return before dark, I grabbed my water, my headlamp, and the heart-stone. I set out weak-legged with hunger, the heart-stone's jagged weight pressed against my left hip. I detoured just far enough to handle my one obligation, my daily visit to my "buddy pile."

To ensure everyone fasting stayed safe—or didn't languish with a broken bone for too many hours, at least—we had a check-in system not unlike a mailbox flag. Our group was an odd number of participants, so three of us in my desert neighborhood had agreed to be buddies. Before we started our fasts, we'd tagged a flat sandstone the size of a picnic table and each picked a distinctive rock to place on its top. Once each day at a designated hour, one of us trekked to our buddy pile, removed the rock from the person who'd been there before us, and set our own rock in its place. That way, if any of us arrived and found the wrong rock on display, we'd know the third buddy hadn't come and likely needed help.

My turn at the buddy pile came late each afternoon. I needed to check in on the way to the sentinel stones because I might not be able to find it in the dusk on the way back. As I approached it, something looked off. When I spied what it was, I burst into tears.

My noon buddy had left, propped against his usual rock, a gray heart-shaped stone fringed in white mineral crystals. It was a miniature of the heart-stone I was about to give up. Grateful for this small sign of approval and compensation, I carefully tucked this gift into my palm. When I asked about it later, my buddy told me, "I'd been carrying that heart around in my pocket for days, but when I visited the buddy pile that afternoon, I thought, 'I'm going to leave this for Joni.'"

Carrying both stone hearts to the sentinel hill, I stopped before the guardian boulders.

"May I pass?" I asked them.

They conferred. Still dubious, they allowed it this time, though I would not have been shocked if the more hostile one had rolled toward me to physically block my path. That one I gave the widest berth I could in the narrow route. (Maybe four days without food had been working on me, but I did write a novel featuring a kid who hears the voices of stones.)

With no trouble other than heavy breathing, I ascended to the hilltop and the sentinels' feet. Their thrust out of the hillside appeared to be natural, but there was no doubt of their role. Atop the lowest and flattest, most table-like, sat an arrow-shaped white crystal as long as my hand. It pointed directly at the pictographs in the distance below.

"Humbly—may I please leave this with you to watch over, too?" I rested Tony's heart-stone at the base of one sentinel, at its back, which was catching the setting sun. Doing so pleased me, and not only because it tended his memory. It helped me feel we were both part of the passage of time, a blip in the panorama those sentinel stones and the pictograph rock had all witnessed. And though our bodies, our footprints, our entwined fingers may be fleeting, our spirits also had an eternal place here, cupped between the stony earth and the embracing sky.

Such a rite probably seems strange to most people. My actions were no more than assigning meaning to rocks—a laugh in a desert spilling over with stones. Emotions were expressed through what was at hand. But building Tony's cairn, pacing around it, scattering it later, and finding the right cache for its most symbolic stone helped me carve a context for my pain, one that was exclusive and unique, like our love. *Special.* Those moments were the most comfort I've found in three years of trying to cope with the loss. My rituals didn't extinguish my grief but allowed it to rest. They also eased my nagging sense I was letting down Tony, not living up to our *carpe diem* spirit.

I couldn't have done it sooner. I wasn't ready. It felt like a passage—evolution if not transformation—and I think back on the site of my cairn with love, not a cringe. Unlike Tony's traditional funeral.

This experience made me realize how few meaningful rituals our lives hold today. My rites in the desert, guided only by instinct and intuition, linked the mundane around me with my emotions and spirit. Bringing these realms together in imaginative actions with rocks helped me feel better equipped to move forward.

Leaving the heart-stone in good care on the hill, I hurried back toward my camp, limping in before dark. The sun set as I watched, my heart full. My solo time would end the next morning, when I'd return to the companionship of our group. Fasting had not delivered a vision, despite the continuous growl of my stomach, but my rituals had been well worth the trip.

Then, about four the next morning, I awoke with a start to weep in gratitude for the vision I'd thought I'd been denied.

Seeing Him When He Moves

During my time in the desert, I enjoyed several dreams that felt helpful, most related to my writing career. Only that one dream near the end, on my last night alone, struck with the significance for me to call it a vision. It began with me peering down into a pool of dark water, where something seemed to shimmer beneath the surface. My view suddenly flipped, disorienting, so I wasn't looking down into water but up into the night sky, the shimmering stars and galaxies of the cosmos.

I raised my arms to it. "Okay, take me. I want to come." I was ready to leave this life and this Earth.

Lifted into space, I arrived on a large gray outcrop of stone. Tony stood on its far end, facing away. I rushed forward to hug him, but before I reached him, he turned, raised one finger to stop me, and said, "Watch this." He leapt sideways. When he landed on another boulder, he'd become a patch of lichen there the size of an egg.

Marveling, I approached and bent to look closer. "Try it," said his voice in my ear. "Life is life." As my finger reached down to touch it, he leapt again, and the lichen was gone. As he moved through the air, I saw him as Tony, but this time he landed in a nearby pool of water, a deep grotto among the stones. He became a small fish in a school of others, though I couldn't tell which one was him.

"Come on in," his voice said. Hesitant, I crouched to test how cold the water might be. When I slipped my hands in—it was cool but not cold—the rest of me flowed effortlessly after. Becoming a fish, too, I joined the others. Morphing from one life form to another without trying struck me as both delightful and funny. In life we had watched fish while scuba diving, and here in what appeared to be the afterlife, we could be the fish, too, to gain their perspective.

Now that I was in the water, however, I could see three much larger jacks hovering in the shadows not far away. *Oh no! I might get eaten.*

Tony's voice reassured me, "Just be a bigger fish." Poof, I was bigger and laughing again as the frightened jacks darted away.

I tried to twist to look up, out of the water, and the effort turned me back into myself, now standing on the far side of the pool. Before me a puzzling scene unfolded—the filming of a movie for which God was the director. It was some kind of thriller. The dark scene unfolding before the cameras was filled with crime and abuse.

Dubious about both the scene being shot and the director, I questioned what I was seeing. "God is a director?" Such a trivial task seemed below the Divine. (The double entendre of the word "director" didn't occur to me until later.) I turned away from the actors, seeking some explanation. Above and to my right, in a shallow cave in a cliff, stood God Himself. A bearded old white guy in a robe, he looked down at me.

This traditional, patriarchal image of God annoyed me. Ridiculous. But there it was. At least He was willing to answer my question and my unspoken dismay about the evil in the movie.

"Yes." His voice was measured, one word at a time. "The mistake people make is thinking I am all good. I am also mean." The word resonated: both lowly and cruel.

"But why?" I asked.

He became a roiling mass of black and gold, like ink being stirred into molten gold. The mass thundered, "Because I also have to destroy!" Churning faster, mixing and checkering more, it advanced toward me. "GOD IS ALL."

Terror woke me, gasping, to the night sky above, whose black space and silver stars were reassuringly still. After a few tears of gratitude, I lay recalling each scene and the wild emotional swings still vibrating in me—the joy of seeing Tony. The delight at our fluid transformations muting the disappointment that he didn't seem to want me to touch him—even when he was lichen! The humor of playing fish before my confusion about the movie turned to dismay, annoyance, and finally fear.

"Life is life." That didn't surprise me. It naturally follows from the evidence that life is a fountain that recycles itself, one life form ending to feed another. The idea that the Divinity is mean, however, sanctifying natural disasters and serial killers, isn't something I was aware I believed. Though it certainly would solve the old problem of evil.

Whether genuine vision or subconscious musing, this dream both reassured and challenged me. If the divine force that sparks all life can be cruel, the implications for hope and free will are big. People value goodness and behavior we call humanist. Can humans aspire to be "better" than God? Or are we nearer the divine image, the All, if we're bad? Are we perhaps even "directed" to be? There aren't answers, of course, but the questions intrigue.

Returning to base camp brought mixed emotions. The avocado half that broke my fast was delicious, but my connection with nature and my own intuition has never felt so strong. That made me loath to end those four days alone. The silence of even a windy desert amplifies our still, small voice inside. The time also convinced me of the value of ritual as a bridge between our physical and imaginative worlds. I began considering how rocks might help serve the same purpose for me at home.

In our post-fast debrief, we shared key experiences so our guides could reflect our own words back at us, often noting the implications. When I shared this dream, our wise cowboy repeated of Tony,

"You'll only see him when he moves." I nodded, hearing the meaning behind my own words. Even with the things I loved most about him returned to the earth with the cairn stones I threw, Tony can move for me still—whether movement is defined as a stroke of financial luck, a prompting to travel, the impulse that draws my gaze to a puddle shaped like a heart, or the dance of a thought in the back of my head that resonates in his voice, not mine.

Bringing Others Along

Apparently I haven't learned everything I am here for. My packing would be easier if I were sure what my suitcase was missing, but intuition has brought me this far. It's guiding my actions forward.

Cultivating my intuition also gives me a purpose. Monks aren't known for proselytizing, but they set an example. Similarly, the more I confess to abandoning reason, the more others become willing to come along with me.

My friend Monica's husband, George, for instance, spent much of his career in mortgage banking—not a profession known for its whimsy. Still, during a recent visit to them, he told me about an incident the previous summer. Although nasty allergic reactions weren't part of his past, an unfriendly bee provoked an anaphylactic crash, which catapulted him into a near-death experience. He described a sense of bliss and of welcoming companions who receded when he was revived.

After meeting Tony, George had envisioned the four of us going diving together. If only. Still, the impossibility is so enticing that I like to imagine Tony among the crowd George encountered.

Synchronicity can become a team sport. My visit with Monica coincided with my birthday. That morning, after she surprised me with gifts and a cake, she asked what we should do to acknowledge Tony that day.

"We could set a place for him at the table," she suggested. "But since we're having dinner in a restaurant tonight, I don't know how that would work." Instead I bought myself a kaleidoscope, calling it a gift from Tony. Its gorgeous mandalas remind me of universal patterns and light.

Then Monica and I drove to visit a mentor of mine who lived not far away. Patti had invited us over for lunch, which we brought from a deli to share with her adorable husband. When we arrived, the table was set with five places. Patti dished tuna salad onto all five plates before realizing there were only four of us present. No others had ever been planned or discussed. With her husband teasing about her ability to count, Patti left the fifth plate on the table.

As we drove away later, Monica exclaimed, "I was biting my tongue the whole time!" We shared teary laughter. Her suggestion for an empty place setting had been granted. I didn't feel Tony's presence there with us, but maybe we saw him in motion. Regardless, I cherish such everyday magic. The chance to share it with somebody else echoes the oneness I had with him.

Postscript to Tony

S o now you know everything, sweetheart. Maybe, in your present form, you didn't need it spelled out, but I did.

When I began writing to share my secret with you, I hoped that confessing my intuitions might make your absence easier to bear. Words on paper felt natural. So much of our relationship was first shaped over email. If I laid out the clues, lining them up like fireflies on a branch, surely they'd expose enough Patterned Mystery to convince me you were waiting for me. That fate is keeping me here for a reason and can also be trusted to reunite us. Any timeframe longer than yesterday chafes, but we rocked a long-distance relationship once. We ought to be able to do it again. The only acceptable excuse if you're not there when I die will be if you've already started the next life we'll share. At the moment I quail at reincarnation, at the likelihood of returning to a less privileged life. Becoming a tree or a dog sounds better. Even embracing the void would hurt less. But another leap into this surging emotion will be worth it if you'll be there feeling it with me.

Despite my hopes, on many days these Greatest Hits of My Heart offer only limited comfort. You're not with me, embodied. Nothing changes that. Little gifts occasionally drop into my life to reinforce my sense that you're still showing me love. But only from afar, and not often enough to sustain me. I may be imitating a monk, but I'd make a bad Buddhist. I still want desire fulfilled, not erased. I go to sleep every night hoping you'll appear in my dreams. I wake each morning, sorry for daylight and heaving a sigh: one more day without you. I'm alive under protest.

Universe: Listen to yourself. Have I not made myself clear you're supposed to be here without Tony?

Me: Maybe so, but don't expect me to cheer. I never promised not to long for the allotted time of my death. Unless that promise is recorded in the Law Offices of Gabriel & Shiva LLC, but if so, I'm not supposed to remember that contract. For the record, though, I've long suspected I would die choking on something.

Universe: (whistles)

Meanwhile, I pretend I'm in the afterlife, following my heart because you reside there, ready to guide me to you. My sense of possibility helps me fend off despair, and heeding my intuition, I act. On sad days, my hope and my energy flag. On better days I try to make up the slack. I know that's what you'd want. It's not what I want; I'd rather be dead than feel this cavernous loss for the rest of my life. But sometimes love is doing what your partner wants. Even if they're not here anymore.

The more tightly I hold non-rational claims of the spirit, the less gloom overtakes me—and the more fireflies appear on my path. I find flashes of our life together, bursts of the joy and excitement and love. They most often come when I'm running or walking. The cast of light through the leaves, the rippling river, an unripe wild apple on the trail prompts a memory, a glimpse—

Plums dropped on a trail beside Idaho's Snake River.

We located the tree and you picked one for me. That plum whispers of our campsite in a California orange grove.

Your long arm reaching high to a half-dozen fat oranges, which had to be cradled in the tail of my shirt because they wouldn't fit in my arms.

From there I flash to Hawaii.

Pausing on the driveway of our B&B to pluck fingerling bananas from the tree by the gate.

These chains of memory come so rapid-fire they could be a subtle slippage of time. For an instant we are together again.

Like a wandering monk, I chase after that altered state on my feet. When I'm lucky, it refracts me through the waters of time and back to our infinite moment of love. The rest of the time, I touch you through my heart, feeling your masculine presence within me and holding open the possibility you can influence my world. Imagination lifts me above earthly limits and helps create meaning my life would otherwise lack. Meanwhile, intuition is the sense that connects us beyond death, the spiritual connection that keeps our love close.

Coda

My dearest reader who is still alive,

Consider this your encounter with the Universe.
You can have this. But you will lose it.
Whoever, whatever you love, it will pass. Act accordingly.
You could worry. You could cling and maybe suffocate the love. Or you can cherish. *Prioritize.* Who gives a shit about the dirty dishes in the sink? (If your loved one cares, you still might want to do them. Tony would call it an act of lovemaking, which is an excellent priority.)
Pay attention to your heart. Let it feel the weight of possibilities, the tugging current of fate. Don't let anyone shame you for honoring truths of your spirit. Follow your intuition and act.

"We must remember that the rationalistic attitude of the West is not the only possible one and is not all-embracing, but is in many ways a prejudice and a bias that ought perhaps to be corrected."
—Carl G. Jung

Endnotes and Permissions

1. Hanagarne, Josh. *The World's Strongest Librarian*. New York: Avery/Penguin, 2013. p. 266

2. Lankshear, Colin, and McLaren, Peter. *The Politics of Liberation: Paths from Freire*. Abingdon (UK): Routledge, 2002. p. 27

About the Author

Joni Sensel is the author of more than a dozen nonfiction titles for adults and five novels for young readers, including a Junior Library Guild selection. She holds an MFA in writing from Vermont College of Fine Arts (2015) and has served in leadership roles for the Society of Children's Book Writers & Illustrators (SCBWI). Over the past twenty years, Sensel has taught dozens of writing workshops and seminars in locations from Alaska to Amsterdam. A certified grief educator and trained First Aid Arts responder, she has recently focused her teaching on creativity and spirituality. Sensel's adventures have taken her to the corners of fifteen countries, the heights of the Cascade Mountains, the length of an Irish marathon, and the depths of love. She lives at the knees of Mount Rainier in Washington State with a puppy who came into her life as a gift that reflected afterlife influence.

SELECTED TITLES FROM SHE WRITES PRESS

She Writes Press is an independent publishing company founded to serve women writers everywhere. Visit us at www.shewritespress.com.

Filling Her Shoes: Memoir of an Inherited Family by Betsy Graziani Fasbinder $16.95, 978-1-63152-198-0
A "sweet-bitter" story of how, with tenderness as their guide, a family formed in the wake of loss and learned that joy and grief can be entwined cohabitants in our lives.

Fire Season: A Memoir by Hollye Dexter $16.95, 978-1-63152-974-0
After she loses everything in a fire, Hollye Dexter's life spirals downward and she begins to unravel—but when she finds herself at the brink of losing her husband, she is forced to dig within herself for the strength to keep her family together.

Splitting the Difference: A Heart-Shaped Memoir by Tré Miller-Rodríguez $19.95, 978-1-938314-20-9
When 34-year-old Tré Miller-Rodríguez's husband dies suddenly from a heart attack, her grief sends her on an unexpected journey that culminates in a reunion with the biological daughter she gave up at 18.

This Trip Will Change Your Life: A Shaman's Story of Spirit Evolution by Jennifer B. Monahan $16.95, 978-1-63152-111-9
One woman's inspirational story of finding her life purpose and the messages and training she received from the spirit world as she became a shamanic healer.

Where Have I Been All My Life? A Journey Toward Love and Wholeness by Cheryl Rice $16.95, 978-1-63152-917-7
Rice's universally relatable story of how her mother's sudden death launched her on a journey into the deepest parts of grief—and, ultimately, toward love and wholeness.

Seeing Red: A Woman's Quest for Truth, Power, and the Sacred by Lone Morch $16.95, 978-1-938314-12-4
One woman's journey over inner and outer mountains—a quest that takes her to the holy Mt. Kailas in Tibet, through a seven-year marriage, and into the arms of the fierce goddess Kali, where she discovers her powerful, feminine self.